From a Member of the Audience

In Loving Memory of My Parents
Wayne L and Marjorie M Gregory

From a Member of the Audience
Memories of Over Fifty Years
By Wayne L Gregory
With a Foreword by Charles W. Gregory, his son

Published by **CWG Press**,
1517 NE 5th Terrace, Apt 1, Fort Lauderdale, FL 33304

copyright 2016 by Charles W. Gregory

ALL RIGHTS RESERVED

978-0-9906714-3-5

Foreword

How can I describe Wayne L Gregory? He was my dad.

He loved the theater. I don't think I've ever known anyone for whom theater was such an important part of life. One might safely say it *was* his life. Not that he didn't love my mother with all his heart; not that he didn't love me.

My parents used to love to tell people at parties that they'd been married on the 3rd of March and I came along on the 23rd. Then they'd reveal the seven-year gap in between... In the fifties in the USA such things were far more important than they are today, and they managed to shock people quite effectively. Which of course was a little bit of theater on their own part.

Dad taught for 37 years at Walnut Hills High School in Cincinnati. He'd planned to retire after 40 years, in a year that would also feature my graduation from the same school and the 25th Wedding Anniversary of my mom and dad. That didn't quite work out, as we moved to Philadelphia 3 years before that long-planned festive year, mostly because of issues I was having... it's not easy to attend the same school where your father teaches, for one thing. Or to be the only child of parents who are significantly older than those of nearly all your peers.

For that long run at Walnut Hills, Dad directed two plays every year as well as teaching speech and drama as part of the English Department. It was one of the earliest schools in the country to draw advanced students from all over a city in order to prepare them for college. Dad's productions sold out their performances and were reviewed – nearly always favorably -- by the same critics who wrote up the big-name touring companies that visited Cincinnati. I wouldn't say he was a celebrity but he was certainly well respected in the area.

Perhaps nothing I write can describe my father any better than this newspaper article from April 21, 1966:

> The Script Is 'Harvey' ... but Mr. Gregory loves classics, too.
>
> The Play's The Thing Teacher-Director Sees Theatrics As Helpful To Students
>
> BY BOB WEBB Cincinnati Enquirer Education Writer
>
> If Shakespearean plays live on in Cincinnati high schools, one reason may be Wayne L. Gregory. As play director at Walnut Hills High School, he's kept a terrapin-like grip on the classics when others would shunt them aside for more modern fare. "A classic is a play that's been able to last through the years, and has something to offer the public which is unusual," said Mr. Gregory, 62, relaxing in the faculty lounge Tuesday. It's not that he objects to the modern, lighter stuff. For that matter, he's pot "Harvey" on tap for 8 p. m.

Friday in the Walnut Hills auditorium. And, well . . . "Harvey," as anyone knows, is as contemporary as the psychiatrist's couch. "We have one classical play, and one non-classic every year," noted Mr. Gregory, in the softly modulated tones of the English, speech and dramatics teacher. "Harvey" is done by juniors. But the fall play at Walnut Hills Is mostly a senior production. Shakespeare's been his classical favorite. He can rip off such titles as "Twelfth Night," "As You Like It," and "Much Ado About Nothing," in the repertoire of plays at Walnut Hills the last 10 or 15 years. "BUT WE do other classics too," observed Mr. Gregory, who joined the Walnut Hills faculty in 1930. "For example, we've done George Bernard Shaw's 'St. Joan.' " And he's quite certain Thornton Wilder's "Our Town." which he revives every few years, ranks as a classic. For all their entertainment value, plays often perform a life-shaping purpose for their performers, Mr. Gregory said. "I have known youngsters who have been problem people before they had parts in plays," he recalled. "They simply were having no fun here as students. Then comes the parts that change their whole lives." He also directs plays at Cincinnati Country Day School. And for seven years he directed summer stock productions at a Culver, Ind., theater no longer operating. He also handled box office chores for University of Cincinnati's "Musickaravan" at Daytona Beach, Fla. In 1964. And last summer he was treasurer for the Traverse City, Mich. Cherry County Playhouse box office. "I've never done any acting, except in a small way in college," noted Mr. Gregory. But if he's never been an actor, like the successful football coach who never played he's known how to pick 'em. "I look over my students in the 10th grade," Mr. Gregory confided, "and from the talent I sense, I plan the plays."

I was blessed to have two wonderful parents, Wayne L. and Marjorie M. Gregory, who loved me without exception or question. When my mom died at age 97 in 2013, I found the vignettes among the boxes of papers and photos that I inherited. I was overjoyed to see my dad's manuscript after all those years, and I vowed to publish it. Finally, three years later, I'm ready to do so.

Without further ado, I am proud to share with the world my father's vignettes, *From a Member of the Audience*.

Chuck Gregory, June 15, 2016, Fort Lauderdale, FL

To Marjorie

with love---

PREFACE

The vignettes which follow are divided into two parts. Part One includes those actors and actresses who are no longer living, and those who are in retirement. Part Two includes those who are still very much with us.

The writing has been done over a period of several years, and, therefore, some of the dates which were accurate, say in 1965, will not be accurate today in 1971. However, I cannot see that this will make very much difference. It is the actors and actresses who will live again in my memory that really matter.

My interest in the theatre covers a period of nearly sixty years. It all began when my grandfather Merchant took me to see two performances, UNCLE TOM'S CABIN and POLLY OF THE CIRCUS, at the old Grand Opera House in Peoria, Illinois. Shortly after these two treats, the opera house burned down and on its site now stands the City Jail. Needless to say I was very young, and my only memory of UNCLE TOM is of the final curtain when Topsy hung on as it went up for the curtain calls. Of POLLY, I remember that she made her first entrance riding a white horse. Research tells me that either Edith or Mabel Talliferro appeared as Polly, as both were on tour at this time.

The years went by and I saw as many plays and musicals as I could, in the United States, in London, Paris and Edinburgh. Many of the theatres in the United States which are mentioned here have long gone out of existence. To name only a few, there were the Empire and New Amsterdam in New York, the Powers, Colonial, and Illinois in Chicago, the Grand Opera House in Cincinnati, and, of course, the Majestic and Orpheum in Peoria.

I would like to mention, also, a list of favorites not only of vaudeville but also of the various Supper Clubs of bygone days as well as those who are still very much with us now. List "A" will include those who either are no longer living or have retired. List "B" will include those who are still very well-known performers today.

List "A": Belle Baker, Nora Banes, George Beban, Lucienne Boyer, Julian Eltinge, Ruth Etting, Judy Garland, Libby Holman, Grace La Rue, Sir Harry Lauder, Jessie Matthews, Bill Robinson, Blossom Seeley, Valeska Surratt, and Frances White.

List "B": Pearl Bailey, Harry Belafonte, Marlene Dietrich, Ella Fitzgerald, Burl Ives, and Ruby Keeler.

Then, too, there are several very great actresses who come within the years these pages cover; however, since I was unable to be in New York when they were playing, I was never able to see them. This is one of my very great regrets. These include Viola Allen, Blanche Bates, Alexandra Carlisle, Marie Doro, Eleanora Duse, Josephine Hull, and Vivien Leigh.

I have gained a great deal of personal enjoyment in writing these essays. It is my hope that others may enjoy them, too. For over twenty-five years my wife has been the other half of "two on the aisle", and none of these writings would ever have been possible without her wise guidance and her careful editing.

Philadelphia,
Pennsylvania
1971

INDEX

Part One

Adams, Maude	1
Anglin, Margaret	4
Arliss, George	6
Bacon, Frank	7
Bainter, Fay	9
Bankhead, Tallulah	12
Banks, Leslie	15
Barrymore, Ethel	16
Barrymore, John	21
Barrymore, Lionel	22
Bennett, Richard	24
Bergner, Elizabeth	26
Bernhardt, Sarah	28
Blinn, Holbrook	29
Boland, Mary	30
Brady, Alice	32
Braithwaite, Lillian	33
Brice, Fannie	34
Burke, Billie	35
Burns, David	37
Byington, Spring	39
Calhern, Louis	40
Cantor, Eddie	41

Chatterton, Ruth	42
Christians, Mady	43
Claire, Ina	45
Cohan, George M.	47
Collier, Constance	49
Collinge, Patricia	51
Compton, Fay	53
Cooper, Gladys	54
Cornell, Katharine	55
Cowl, Jane	62
Craven, Frank	65
Crews, Laura Hope	67
Davies, Gwen Ffrangcon	69
Diggs, Dudley	70
Donahue, Jack	71
Eagles, Jeanne	72
Evans, Edith	74
Ferguson, Elsie	75
Fiske, Mrs.	77
Frederick, Pauline	79
George, Grace	81
Gillette, William	83
Gish, Dorothy	84
Gish, Lillian	84
Greenstreet, Sydney	88
Hajos, Mitzi	91

Hampden, Walter	93
Harding, Anne	96
Hardwicke, Sir Cedric	97
Held, Anna	98
Hitchcock, Raymond	99
Hodge, William	100
Hopkins, Miriam	101
Howard, Leslie	103
Hull, Henry	106
Hunter, Glenn	108
Huston, Walter	110
Inescort, Frieda	112
Janis, Elsie	113
Jolson, Al	114
Kennedy, Madge	115
Larrimore, Francine	117
Laughton, Charles	119
Lawrence, Gertrude	120
Le Gallienne, Eva	123
Leontovich, Eugenie	128
Lillie, Beatrice	130
Lord, Pauline	134
Lunts, The	136
Martin, Vivian	142
Massey, Raymond	143
Maude, Cyril	145

Menken, Helen	146
Merrivale, Philip	148
Miller, Marilyn	150
Morgan, Frank	152
Morgan, Helen	153
Morris, Chester	154
Muni, Paul	156
Nazimova, Alla	158
Ney, Marie	160
Nugent, Elliot	161
O'Neill, Nance	164
Patterson, Elizabeth	165
Pennington, Ann	167
Perkins, Osgood	168
Power, Tyrone, Jr.	169
Printemps, Yvonne	171
Rambeau, Marjorie	173
Rathbone, Basil	175
Reed, Florence	178
Rennie, James	182
Robeson, Paul	185
Robson, May	187
Sanderson, Julia	189
Scheff, Fritzi	191
Segal, Vivienne	193
Skinner, Otis	195
Starr, Frances	197

Stone, Fred	199
Sullavan, Margaret	201
Taylor, Laurette	203
Tempest, Marie	205
Thorndyke, Dame Sybil	207
Tobin, Genevieve	208
Tucker, Sophie	209
Ulric, Lenore	211
Walker, June	213
Warfield, David	215
Waters, Ethel	217
Whitty, Dame May	220
Whiffen, Mrs. Thomas	221
Winwood, Estelle	223
Wood, Peggy	226
Wright, Haidee	228
Wynn, Ed	229
Wynward, Diana	231
Young, Roland	234

FROM A MEMBER OF THE AUDIENCE

MEMORIES OF OVER FIFTY YEARS

by Wayne L. Gregory

MAUDE ADAMS

My first memory of Miss Adams recalls a pair of tickets which were prominently displayed on the side-board in our dining-room at home in Peoria, Illinois. This must have been during the season of 1912-1913, when she was on tour of the United States. The play was PETER PAN and my mother had purchased the tickets early as they were always hard to get. I was ten years old. A few days before the performance I was playing baseball in the yard and I was hit in the eye with a wild pitch. As I wore glasses at this time it was very serious, and I was rushed to the hospital. I never saw PETER PAN.

Five years later, in the spring of 1918, I first saw Maude Adams in A KISS FOR CINDERELLA. This was also in Peoria, at the Orpheum Theatre. Our regular theatre, the Majestic, was being renovated and the road shows were given in what was usually considered our vaudeville theatre. I recall very little of this performance except the scene in the hospital when "Cinderella" was reunited with her "Prince Charming", the policeman.

The next time I saw Miss Adams was in February, 1932, at the Grand Theatre in Cincinnati. She was now out of her long retirement and she was playing Portia in THE MERCHANT OF VENICE. Her co-star was Otis Skinner. The tremendous ovation that she received upon her first entrance still rings in my ears. I was completely captivated by her throaty voice and the illusion of youth that she created. This was on opening night and I went back again the following Friday night to be thrilled all over again. While she was never considered to be a great Portia, she was a winning one.

I heard all of her radio broadcasts which she gave in the following few months of 1932 and 1933. At least the voice was still able to excite me. Most remembered were THE LITTLE MINISTER and WHAT EVERY WOMAN KNOWS.

The last time that I saw Maude Adams was on her lecture tour (by now she was on the faculty of Stephens College in Columbia, Missouri). This occurred at the Taft Theatre in Cincinnati. During the lecture she gave many excerpts from her long and illustrious career, and these were the highlights of the evening. It was a very fitting farewell. A friend of mine had the honor of introducing her, since our mayor, who was supposed to have had the honor, was in the hospital. I recall that the weather was very bad and we were having a blizzard so the audience was small, but we all gave her a warm welcome.

I have always adored her; and, later, in Carmel, California, I had the great good fortune to meet her. She was on vacation and we happened to be staying at the same hotel. Her travelling companion had a son whom I had met on the beach. It was through him that the meeting was arranged. The short half hour or so that I spent in her suite will always remain in my memory. She was gracious and charming in her simplicity, and somehow she had lost much of her shyness.

On the wall of my den, I have a very valuable picture of Miss Adams which was willed to me by an old family friend who had worshipped her for a great number of years. The picture is at least sixty-five years old.

Naturally it has a valued place in my possessions.

Miss Adams died on 17 July, 1953.

MARGARET ANGLIN

Perhaps the best way to describe the greatness of Margaret Anglin is to use a quote from LIFE printed in 1920. It goes: "At all times one finds Miss Anglin displaying perfect control, but with a speed and intensity which are at times terrifying."

I first saw Miss Anglin on 28 December, 1921, at the Princess Theatre in Chicago. The play was THE WOMAN OF BRONZE. It was a terrific evening in the theatre for me. I had never seen a great emotional actress before. I was left limp at the final curtain, as were most of the rest of the audience who were much older than I. I have never forgotten the scene with her husband after her discovery of his infidelity when she almost literally destroys the statue. This was great acting.

Nearly two years later, on 1 October, 1923, when she was on tour across the country, I saw it again at the Majestic Theatre in Peoria. This time I took my mother, and we were both thrilled all over again.

The next time I saw Margaret Anglin was on 24 January, 1924, at the Majestic Theatre in Peoria. I was now a senior in high school, and as I recall I took my best girl friend of the moment and splurged, because we sat downstairs in the orchestra. The play was A CHARMING CONSCIENCE. It was on its pre-Broadway tour. It wasn't much of a play, but it did show the other side of Miss Anglin's great ability as an actress. It was a sophisticated comedy of manners. She was excellent, and she seemed to be enjoying herself.

Ten years passed by before I saw her again and unfortunately it was for the last time. This was on New Year's Eve, 1933, at the Cox Theatre in Cincinnati. The play was HER MASTERS' VOICE, and she was as delightful and witty as always. I still believe this comedy is one of the best of all the comedies of the 1930's. In her cast was Queenie Smith, whom I had seen in musicals. She, too, was very funny.

Miss Anglin was in and out of retirement for the next few years, but I never saw her again. Even in the present day of our fine actresses, I feel that she has had no equal, unless it would be Judith Anderson. She died quietly, in retirement, in January, 1958.

GEORGE ARLISS

There was an elusive quality about George Arliss. He was a thin man of medium height, with a very expressive face. He was a very fine actor, but he seemed cold and austere. He expressed very little emotion.

I first saw Mr. Arliss on 12 December, 1920, at the Majestic Theatre in Peoria. The play was JACQUES DUVAL, a play adapted from the French by George Kaufman. It told the story of a French doctor falsely accused of malpractice, and of his being able to regain his standing as a prominent physician. His leading lady was the beautiful and talented Elizabeth Risdon.

I next saw him on 29 January, 1926, at the Adelphi Theatre in Chicago. The play was OLD ENGLISH by John Galsworthy. This was a "tour de force" for Mr. Arliss--almost a one man show which told of a stubborn British peer who preferred to die with "his boots on". The final scene, when the wines and a special dinner that he had demanded, against his doctor's orders, finally bring on his death, was a great one to remember.

I saw George Arliss for the last time on 15 October, 1928, at the Shubert Theatre in Cincinnati. The play was THE MERCHANT OF VENICE. His Shylock was suave, cunning, and completely without sympathy. The Portia was Frieda Inescort.

George Arliss was very active in the films, also. I remember him most in DISRAELI. Here he gave perhaps the finest performance of his long career. He died on 5 February, 1946, in his native England.

FRANK BACON

I search for adjectives to describe Frank Bacon, but none seem to suffice. So I will just remember him as a most lovable old man. Long years of frustration and poor roles, years in which he had never really been recognized, were finally brought to an end when he appeared in LIGHTNIN', a play which was written for his special talents.

I saw him as Lightnin' Bill at the Blackstone Theatre in Chicago, first on 18 December, 1921, and then again on 14 January, 1922. There was something warm and human about his acting. There was also something peculiarly American in his plight, and in the clever manner in which he outwitted his enemies. Everyone in the audience seemed to associate him with a grandfather image, or at least with what one wished his grandfather had been. It was a special charm and a winsome quality that was all his own that endeared him to everyone who ever saw him. He died while playing this role, which he had been playing for over four years, and at his death one realized how long he had been waiting for this chance. I shall never forget the pure entertainment that he gave to me as a high school student, who was stage struck at a very early age. Even now, over forty-five years later, there are moments in this fond and foolish old play that remain very clear in my memory. His supporting cast included: Mildred Booth, Jane Oaker, and, most interesting, the young Jason Robards who is the father of one of our most important actors today.

Frank Bacon is a cherished memory. One other memory I must add here. He came to Peoria during the last weeks that he was alive to be the guest of the Mayor and other dignitaries when the road company of LIGHTNIN' was in town, with Thomas Jefferson in the leading role. There was a reception afterwards and, through friends of my family, we were invited. It was a great evening, and I had the good fortune to shake his hand.

FAY BAINTER

Fay Bainter has had a long and very versatile career in the theatre, from musical comedy to serious roles. In each she has given a quality of honesty and sureness. I do not recall her as a great actress in the same sense that others have been, but I remember with pleasure the times that I have seen her. It has been over thirty years since I last saw her, so that my memories may not be as fresh as for other actresses I've seen more recently.

I saw her first, my scrap books tell me, on 1 January, 1922, at the Majestic Theatre in Peoria. The play with music was EAST IS WEST. It was one of her most famous roles and she had played it up and down these United States. Her Ming Toy was full of charm, and her youthful singing voice was pure and clear.

The next time that I saw her was on 2 March, 1925, at the Studebaker Theatre in Chicago. This was another play with music, THE DREAM GIRL. Walter Wolf was her co-star, and I have but the very vaguest memories of this performance. I do recall, however, that I was drawn to the theatre to see Fay Bainter because of some very interesting stories that had been going the rounds of the college that I was attending at that time. It seems that our football coach, who shall be nameless here, had come from the same home town in Iowa that Miss Bainter had, and all of his life he had been in love with her. She, however, preferred having her career instead of becoming the wife of a college football coach, and neither had ever married. How true was this story, I have no proof; but it was a good story, and they remained close friends, and he did go to Chicago whenever she played there. This much I know is true, because he was in the audience for this performance the night that I was there.

The next time that I saw Miss Bainter was in December of 1930, at the 44th Street Theatre in New York. This was in a revival of LYSISTRATA which had been put on first in Philadelphia and had caught on, and when it came into New York it found a large and appreciative audience and had a long run. Miss Bainter played Kalonika, the young girl, and she gave a beautiful performance. The play had Blanche Yurka in the title role, and Ernest Truex as the husband. It was hilarious and bawdy, but fun.

I saw her next on 26 October, 1926, at the Grand Theatre in Cincinnati. The play was another revival. This time it was Barrie's THE ADMIRABLE CHRICHTON. She was Lady Mary. Here she was very ably supported by Walter Hampden and Sydney Greenstreet, as Chrichton and Lord Loam respectively. Her performance was good, but she did not always create the feeling of the snobbish Lady Mary. She was at her best in the middle of the play, when they were on the island and she could be more realistic in character.

Fortunately, the last time that I saw Fay Bainter was in one of her very best roles. This was at the Shubert Theatre in New York during the season of 1935. The play was, of course, DODSWORTH. Her characterization of Fran Dodsworth, the midwestern shrew, was a masterful job. She had finally come into her own as a very fine dramatic actress. She gave the role all of her best talents and, along with these, a definite feeling for the woman she was playing. She matched Walter Huston in every way; it was a great achievement. I shall long remember the accuracy with which she played this difficult role to an American audience that had such definite opinions about this character because of the very popular novel from which the play was dramatized. She _was_ Fran Dodsworth! I am happy, now that she is in retirement, that at least once in her career she was able to play a role that was equal to her unique ability.

Miss Bainter died in 1968.

TALLULAH BANKHEAD

Of all the American actresses who have reached the top of their profession, and then have allowed themselves to waste their talents, no one is more guilty than Miss Bankhead. This has been a great loss to our theatre, when we have so few who have really great talent. Tallulah Bankhead had been in several roles in New York, and she had had a very successful London career, before I ever had a chance to see her.

I saw her first on 22 February, 1937, at the Cox Theatre in Cincinnati. The play was REFLECTED GLORY. In this she appeared as an actress somewhat down on her luck. Her leading man was Clay Clement. The play was not great, but her personality came through, and it was an entertaining evening in the theatre. I decided to play a "wait and see" game before I came to any decision about Miss Bankhead as an actress.

I didn't have to wait long, for the following fall, on a pre-Broadway tour, Miss Bankhead brought her production of Shakespeare's ANTONY AND CLEOPATRA to Cincinnati. I saw it at the Cox Theatre on 1 November, 1937. Tallulah Bankhead was in no way ready to attempt the most difficult of all of the Shakespearean heroines. This was perhaps the most flagrant example of misguided casting that I can recall. I do not go quite as far in condemning her as some of the New York reviewers did a few weeks later, because she did have her moments. In spite of everything that was wrong with the performance, she did manage to create, near the end, a very moving death scene. However, as a whole she lacked the regal quality of the queen, and she lacked, too, the passion that the role must have. Conway Tearle, brought out of retirement after his somewhat inadequate performance in DINNER AT EIGHT a few seasons back, was equally miscast as Antony. I remained still hopeful to "wait and see".

Two years later I saw Miss Bankhead in perhaps her greatest performance. And, as far as I am concerned, she made up for all of the other times that I had seen her. This was, of course, in THE LITTLE FOXES. I saw it on 19 June, 1939, at the National Theatre in New York. Her performance as Regina was filled with malevolence, with perfect timing, and with all of the other things which make great theatre. Frank Conway and Patricia Collinge were her equals in every way. These three made it a thrilling experience in the theatre.

I next saw Miss Bankhead on the opening night of THE SKIN OF OUR TEETH, at the National Theatre in Washington, D. C. This was on 9 November, 1942. Thornton Wilder's tragi-comic allegory of the problems that have faced the world since it began gave her a chance to show again her real talent and to show her great versatility. As Sabina, she was in her element, both physically and histrionically. It was a performance to remember. The Marches (Frederic and Florence), along with Florence Reed, Frances Heflin, and Montgomery Clift, were with her.

Three years later I saw her again, at the National Theatre in Washington, D. C. The date was 26 February, 1945. The play was FOOLISH NOTION. Although it was written by Philip Barry especially for Miss Bankhead, it was not one of his better plays. It seemed to lack substance, and its theme and premise were never very clearly stated. However, it was a fun evening, and Miss Bankhead did have a good part. She had quite a remarkable cast with her; it included Henry Hull, Donald Cook, Aubrey Mather, and Mildred Dunnock. Also in the cast, in a small role, was Mary Barthelmess, daughter of Richard Barthelmess, a silent film star of wide fame.

The next time that I saw Tallulah Bankhead she, along with Donald Cook, was having a field day with Noel Coward's PRIVATE LIVES. This was at the Harris Theatre in Chicago, on 11 August, 1947. Here she was more the personality than the actress; and while she made Amanda more of a caricature than the character as Mr. Coward had written it, she was very amusing.

Many years went by before I saw her again. In fact, it was sixteen years. These years were filled with films, radio, T. V. appearances, none of which added to her stature as an actress. I saw her for the last time on 27 April, 1963, at the Shubert Theatre in Cincinnati. For reasons that I will never understand, she chose to revive a weak little comedy called HERE TODAY. I had seen it thirty-odd years before, with Ruth Gordon, and even then it wasn't much of a comedy. This time it was even weaker, and it was very dated. She did all that she could with it, but there was little that could make it come alive. She did have Estelle Winwood with her; and she wisely gave the entire show over to Miss Winwood, a very great comedienne, so that the show wasn't a total loss. Miss Bankhead was a bit heavier than I had remembered her, but she still had her moments of glamour.

Of all her films, I recall LIFEBOAT with pleasure as a fine piece of acting, and A ROYAL SCANDAL as one of the funniest film I have ever seen.

Tallulah Bankhead isn't much in the news these days. Maybe she will again give us one more of her really fine performances. Let us hope so.

Miss Bankhead died in 1970.

LESLIE BANKS

The death, a few years ago, of Leslie Banks brought him very vividly to my mind. Although I had seen him only three times over a period of ten years, there was always something about him that I admired. Perhaps it was a solid quality, and a very resonant speaking voice.

I saw Mr. Banks first at the Princess Theatre in Chicago, on 28 December, 1929. The play was THE INFINITE SHOEBLACK, in which he was co-starred with Helen Menken. It was a strange play, about man's unhappiness in seeking the unattainable in life. I recall that he was very moving in the role.

I saw him next, again in Chicago but this time at the Erlanger Theatre, on 2 January, 1938. The play was WINE OF CHOICE. Here he was co-starred with Miriam Hopkins. This was a very amusing comedy, and he was excellent opposite the glamorous Miss Hopkins.

The last time that I saw Leslie Banks was a little over a year and a half later, in July, 1939. This was at the New Theatre in London. The play was THE MAN IN HALFMOON STREET. He was supported by Ann Todd. This was a typical summer mystery play, so dear to the hearts of London theatre-goers. It was one of those plays in which the major character changes his role from the suave British gentleman to a man of evil. It was a tour de force for Mr. Banks, and it showed his versatility, but little else.

I was sorry that he had left the cast of LOST IN THE STARS before I saw that beautiful musical play. I am sure that his performance as the father of the boy who was murdered by the Negro must have been one of his best.

ETHEL BARRYMORE

The haunting beauty and the loveliness of Miss Barrymore will remain as one of my most cherished memories. Her voice was like a cello, and the little way she had of tossing her head is another fond recollection.

I first saw Ethel Barrymore on 23 April, 1919, from a hard-earned seat in the gallery of the Majestic Theatre in Peoria. The play was THE OFF CHANCE. Her leading man was William Boyd, and my program tells me that in the cast was the young Eva Le Gallienne. The play was a mere trifle, and I do not recall too much of its plot. However, I do remember the final line, after her leading man had said, "Perhaps we shall meet in heaven," and she answered, "I don't think I would consider it an appointment." Somehow this has remained with me. In those days, I worked hard after school in a grocery store, and in the evenings I was an usher in the Apollo Theatre (movie theatre) to earn my spending money. Therefore, the next time that I saw her was from an orchestra seat in the old Powers Theatre in Chicago. This was in October 1920 and the play was DECLASSEE by Zoe Akins. Lady Helen was one of her most famous roles, and the play had heartbreak and exciting drama. She was at her best and I loved it. Henry Daniell was her leading man.

The next time that I saw Miss Barrymore was in the spring of 1924, at the Orpheum Theatre in Peoria. Once again the Majestic was undergoing renovations. The play was THE LAUGHING LADY. It was a frolicsome romp with little substance, but it was my adored Miss B. One of my most unforgettable memories was her performance of Paula in THE SECOND MRS. TANQUERAY which comes next on my list. The date was in January of 1925, the theatre, the Blackstone in Chicago. I was in college now, Northwestern, and the theatre was near at hand. One memory of this performance was the time when she sat down at the piano to play softly and Caley's line to Aubrey Tanqueray, "How wretched she looks" was very meaningful. Again, in the final act, when she reminds Aubrey of the list of names she had brought him on the night before they were married--this, too, was heartbreaking. Henry Daniell was again her leading man.

In 1926 she took a "busman's holiday", and trouped up and down the land in the vaudeville houses with a revival of Barrie's THE TWELVE POUND LOOK. I caught it at the Palace Theatre in Chicago. Her Kate was a classic, and I recall every line with relish. (I only wish I could have seen her final performance in New York, when she revived it again for the ANTA Album at its benefit performance on 29 January, 1950. I would like to have been a part of that audience, when they gave her a five minute ovation as she made her first appearance.)

The next time I saw Ethel Barrymore was on 11 April, 1928. Because the show had closed its Chicago engagement before I could get to see her, I dashed up to Milwaukee, Wisconsin, where at the Pabst Theatre I saw her in THE CONSTANT WIFE. Her leading men were Henry Daniell and Frank Conroy. As Constance she was at her charming best. She had few rivals when it came to sophisticated comedy. Mr. Maugham had written a delightful play, full of irony and scintillating wit.

In September, 1928, I moved to Cincinnati, where I lived for nearly forty years. In the years from 1929 to the late thirties, she came often to our town. She played at the Shubert Theatre. There were four plays here over several years. First: the duo, THE KINGDOM OF GOD and THE LOVE DUEL. These are the plays with which she opened her own theatre in

New York which still proudly bears her name. Her leading men were Louis Calhern and McKay Morris. Of the two THE KINGDOM OF GOD was the better play. It showed her great versatility and her grasp of character change. THE LOVE DUEL was a pleasing enough comedy with little depth. Next came her revival of THE SCHOOL FOR SCANDAL. She was electric and the screen scene was a delight. Her leading men were Charles H. Crocker-King, Walter Gilbert, and McKay Morris.

Next came one of her only really serious failures. This was SCARLET SISTER MARY. The least said, the better. It was a very poor play, and while Miss Barrymore did all that she could, it never really came alive. It had an interesting cast, however, which included Estelle Winwood and, again, Walter Gilbert. It also had her daughter, Ethel Barrymore Colt, in the cast.

The next time that I saw her I was in New York for the Christmas holidays. I saw THE GHOST OF YANKEE DOODLE written by Sidney Howard, at the Guild Theatre on 27 December, 1937. Her co-star was Dudley Diggs. She was playing the role of Sara Garrison in a play about the political problems involved in appeasement. She had not looked as lovely in several years. The play was not a great success, and it had only a short run. However, it was very meaningful just before the tragedy of the second World War. Frank Conroy was also in the cast.

In the fall of 1938 I saw her in Chicago at the Selwyn Theatre in WHITEOAKS. She had the old charm and grace as the grandmother in a play dramatized from a series of very famous novels about Jalna. However, it was again a poorly written play and only served as a vehicle for her to show her great versatility. Stephen Haggard was Finch, her favorite grandson.

When I saw Sybil Thorndyke and Emlyn Williams in London in the summer of 1939 in Mr. Williams' wonderful play, THE CORN IS GREEN, I was enthralled. Upon returning to the United States I learned that Miss Barrymore's management had been able to secure the play for her, and I felt that at long last she was to come into her own. I was right. The role of Miss Moffat was perfect for her. I saw it first on Easter Monday, 6 April, 1942, at the Cox Theatre in Cincinnati. While her characterization was quite different from Dame Sybil's, and rightly so, it had much more warmth and humility. The curtain line, in the end of Act Two, when she whispered, "Henry, the Eighth" as the young Morgan begins his examination for Oxford, was given with such prideful humor, that I shall never forget it. I saw this play again, after it had been playing in every city in the land, in Washington, D. C. at the National Theatre, in the spring of 1943. I was thrilled all over again, and I cheered loud and long at the final curtain. Richard Waring was the Morgan Evans in both performances. Mildred Dunnock was also in the cast.

The last time that I saw Ethel Barrymore was again in Washington, D. C. at the National Theatre. The date was the fall of 1944, the play, EMBEZZLED HEAVEN. This was the first performance anywhere. It was in many ways a very fitting farewell to her long career. To be able to play the young Teta in Act One (when I knew that she was sixty-five years old) and the pathetic little woman in the last act, when she had the audience with the Pope, was a great achievement. The gracious charm, the cello voice, and the versatility were all intact. It was a great evening.

Yes, I was fortunate to meet Miss Barrymore once. One summer in the early thirties she was visiting the Alfred Wallensteins (he was a cellist with the Chicago Symphony Orchestra). During this time she came once to the opera at Ravinia Park--I had a job there as the assistant box office manager for several summers--and on this particular night my old friend and co-worker, Ray Walsh of Beloit, Wisconsin, dashed into the box office exclaiming, "Wayne, did you know that Ethel Barrymore is in the audience?" Of course I didn't, but I was as excited as he was. Fortunately, Ray knew the Wallensteins casually, and a meeting was arranged. At intermission under the mystical Japanese lanterns that hung from the trees (these always seemed to make Ravinia a little like fairy land), the meeting took place. She was as beautiful as I wanted her to be, she was as gracious and charming as if we were the most important people in the world whom she really wanted to meet. I am sure that I talked too much as I poured out all of my admiration, but it was an evening long to remember. Her beautiful portrait, taken at the height of her career, also hangs in my den, right across from the one of Miss Adams.

One final note: I have always been sorry that I never saw her play any Shakespeare. I understand that her Portia and her Juliet were both very lovely, youthful, and moving. I was in New York on that fatal night when she was so ill with pneumonia. In passing Times Square I looked up at the news cast that runs around the Times Building, and I was startled to read in bold letters, "General MacArthur lands in Leyte--Ethel Barrymore's temperature lower." I am not ashamed that I said a silent prayer. For nearly forty years (1919-1944) she had been my idol, and she had enriched my life with her special magic.

JOHN BARRYMORE

One of the great theatregoing tragedies of my years as a member of the audience was that I never saw John Barrymore in any of his great roles. I did not see JUSTICE, nor did I see his very great HAMLET. I saw him frequently in the films, of course. Of these I remember the most A BILL OF DIVORCEMENT, GRAND HOTEL, and RASPUTIN AND THE EMPRESS.

I saw him only once in the theatre. This was during the holidays of 1939-40 at the Selwyn Theatre in Chicago. The play was MY DEAR CHILDREN. This was a rather stupid little play which he did as his farewell to the stage. However, in spite of all of the ad-libbing and the playing to the audience that he did to excess, I must have chosen one of his "good nights". For a few moments in the second act, when he was telling his daughter (Doris Dudley) of his great successes, he gave a really fine reading of the "Now, I am alone" soliloquy from HAMLET. It was moving and sincere. I remember that I closed my eyes, and I forgot the silly Tyrolean costume that he was wearing, and just listened.

LIONEL BARRYMORE

The rugged masculinity and the expressive face are the things I most remember about Lionel Barrymore. I saw him only twice on the stage, and many times in the movies.

The first time it was my great good fortune to see him in THE COPPERHEAD by Augustus Thomas. This was during the season of 1918-1919, at the Majestic Theatre in Peoria. Because my grandfather had been in the audience at Fords' Theatre in Washington, D. C. on that fatal night of 14 April, 1865 when President Lincoln was assassinated, and because my father, who dallied in dramatics and had given readings from Lincoln's speeches at various amateur theatricals, I was brought up to admire Lincoln greatly. All of this is a preamble to my thrilling experience at seeing this play with Lionel Barrymore. Forty-eight years later it is hard for me to recall much of the performance except the final act, which I have always remembered. In the scene when the happiness of Milt Shank's granddaughter was at stake, there was a very dramatic moment and a letter from Abraham Lincoln to reveal that Shanks was not a traitor. Of course, this was a one night stand, and the house was sold out. I remember, too, that my dad bought the tickets, so that we sat downstairs in the orchestra. Doris Rankin and the young Chester Morris were in the cast. (Incidentally, in the summer of 1966 when I was working at the Cherry County Playhouse in Traverse City, Michigan, I met Chester Morris who was playing there, and we had quite a good talk about his long career, and how I had seen him when he was just beginning at the age of sixteen).

The second time that I saw Lionel Barrymore was on 13 April, 1922, again at the Majestic Theatre in Peoria. The play was THE CLAW by

Bernstein, translated from the French by E. Dunn. The tragedy involved here was about the complete ruination of a man by his wife. The final scene showed Mr. Barrymore at his best, when he was completely broken. The woman was played by Irene Fenwick. She was young and quite lovely, as I recall. She later became Mrs. Lionel Barrymore.

Of all his many films, I recall most vividly A FREE SOUL with Norma Shearer, CAMILLE and MATA HARI with Greta Garbo, and RASPUTIN AND THE EMPRESS in which all of the Barrymores appeared.

Of course I heard him do Scrooge, in Dickens' A CHRISTMAS CAROL, over the radio many times, for he did it every Christmas season.

As I close my chapters on the Barrymores, I can only say how fortunate I was to have seen all of them, and at least Lionel and Ethel when they were at their best.

RICHARD BENNETT

Mr. Bennett had a long and exciting career on the American stage. He had a quality of rugged manliness and a keen understanding of the roles in which he played.

I saw him first on 6 February, 1923, at the Majestic Theatre in Peoria. The play was HE WHO GETS SLAPPED. This play was about a circus clown who was deeply in love with one of the younger members of the troupe. It had a quality of circus life, and the staging of the play was especially interesting for this period in our theatre. His leading lady was Martha Bryan Allen who played Consuello.

The only other time that I saw Richard Bennett was at the Blackstone Theatre in Chicago, on 8 October, 1927. The play was THE BARKER. In this play he portrayed the role of the "con man" of a definitely second- or third-rate travelling company, again in a circus. While there was some similarity in the roles, he made the part of Nat peculiarly his own. He was very excellent in this characterization. It was pure melodrama, but it was great fun to see. He was supported by Marjorie Wood, Owen Davis, Jr. and Helen Flint. I recall, too, that I was so impressed with this show that a week later I took my "best girl friend of the moment" to see it, and we enjoyed it all over again.

His daughters, Constance and Joan, have both carried on the family tradition, and they have both become very accomplished actresses. Joan Bennett I have seen several times, and she has always been very good in the roles that she has played. Constance Bennett was more popular in the films; but she, too, did return to the stage and gave a very fine account of herself in a road company production of AUNTIE MAME. In August of 1965, I read in the news of her very untimely death. Their father, Richard

Bennett, has a definite place in the American Theatre which will not be easy to fill.

Mr. Bennett died in 1969.

ELIZABETH BERGNER

Elizabeth Bergner had been a very popular and much loved actress in Berlin before the 1930's when she played her first role in English. She had also been popular in several well-known films. Her debut in an English-speaking role took place in London in 1934, and she became an overnight sensation.

I remember so well. I was quietly drinking a few beers in the bar of the Kaiserhoff Hotel in Munich, and at the same time reading the London Times. It was July, 1934, and I read that Miss Bergner's long run in London was to come to an end that week. I recall how quickly I dashed to the American Express to book my train and channel passage, so that I could be in London before the week was over. I made it. Naturally the final performances were all sold out. I soon learned of the wonderful London custom of "queuing up" outside the theatre for the gallery seats. I have used this custom many times since, but this very first time was a unique experience. So, after all, I was not disappointed, and I saw Elizabeth Bergner for the first time on Saturday, 28 July, 1934, at the Apollo Theatre in London. The play was ESCAPE ME NEVER. I was thrilled with Miss Bergner, and I have admired her ever since. She has an elfin quality about her which is most appealing. She has, too, a sureness of touch for just the right mood for the role in which she is playing. Her Gemma Jones was filled with pathos and wonder. I recall one moment after the death of her baby, when she crossed the stage to get something out of the dresser drawer, and inadvertently picked up a diaper--no words were spoken, but the memory of that scene has never left me. She was ably supported by Hugh Sinclair and Leon Quartermaine.

I did not see Miss Bergner again until ten years later. By now she had been in America for some time, both in New York in the theatre, and in Hollywood. I saw her on 30 January, 1944, at the Booth Theatre in New York. The play was THE TWO MRS. CARROLLS. This was a mystery play with overtones of frightening suspense. She was charming and gay as the second wife, and her effervescent good humor was even more noticeable in this play. She was beautifully costumed and, in a very special way, very attractive. Victor Jory appeared as the husband, and Irene Worth was also in the cast.

Of her many films, I enjoyed her most in a very amusing comedy about royalty, called CATHERINE, THE GREAT. I also found her delightful as Rosalind in AS YOU LIKE IT, which she played with Laurence Olivier.

I have always been sorry about two things regarding Elizabeth Bergner. The first was that, after she had mastered the English language, she never played, not even for "special performances", any of the great classical roles for which she had been famous in Germany before the war. Second, I was unhappy that her return to the stage in the United States, just a few years ago, was such a failure that she wouldn't even appear in New York, and left the cast while the show was still on the road.

We do not hear very much about her these days, and I suppose that it is doubtful that she will ever come back again. In my opinion, this is a great loss.

SARAH BERNHARDT

On one of her farewell tours during the season of 1916-1917, I was fortunate to see the great Sarah Bernhardt. I saw her from the gallery of the Majestic Theatre in Peoria. At the time, I was thirteen years old.

She had been injured in an automobile accident some time before, and she was now playing only roles in which she could be seated on the stage, or those in which she could recline on a davenport, or, in the case of the last scene, in which she was in a high poster bed.

Not knowing a word of French, I was somewhat at a loss, but I do recall, after all these years, the great depth and power of her voice. She played in HECUBA, a short French play about which I remember nothing, in FIELD OF HONOR, a play about a dying soldier in the First World War, and in the last act of CAMILLE. I recall the final scene the best, since I had heard of the famous old play. The experience is now very dim in my memory fifty years later; however, I have always been glad that I had this chance. I seem to recall, too, that she travelled about the country in her own special Pullman car which was attached to some train, depending upon where she was to appear each night.

HOLBROOK BLINN

Mr. Blinn had been a great character actor for a long period of years, and he was very famous in the silent films long before I saw him for the first and only time on the stage.

This chance came on 10 January, 1926, at the Blackstone Theatre in Chicago. He was co-starred with Judith Anderson in THE DOVE. This was a melodrama of the old West, in which, as the good-bad Mexican bandit, he was at his very best. He had the manner of the old school of acting. He was _the_ star, and there was never a moment in which he didn't make the audience aware of this fact. He was suave, urbane, and he had great personal charm, but as an actor he left much to be desired. I was happy to see him, and I enjoyed his performance very much. My memories of the performance are somewhat vague, except that Miss Anderson was young and vibrant and Holbrook Blinn was static. I recall, too, an amusing moment at the curtain call. Neither would let the other take a single call; and the manner in which they held their hands tightly together, so that neither one could break away, was another example of how Mr. Blinn regarded his position as the star.

MARY BOLAND

Early in July, 1965 I picked up a copy of TIME magazine and read of the death of Mary Boland at the age of eighty. During those eighty years she had given much to the American theatre, and her peculiar sense of comedy technique will be greatly missed. In my opinion she was the last of the great comediennes, and she was in the same class with Laura Hope Crews and Josephine Hull.

My memories of Mary Boland extend over a period of many years. Her knowledge of character and her perfect timing have rarely been equalled. There was something about her mastery of a role which was purely her own. Whenever she came on to a stage there was an electric quality which set off something in the audience and caused almost constant laughter.

I saw her first in THE VINEGAR TREE at the Shubert Theatre in Cincinnati in 1932. This was a very human and amusing comedy. She was at her best in the role of a somewhat confused wife.

I next saw her, again at the Shubert Theatre in Cincinnati, in 1934. This time she was in a musical comedy. Its title was FACE THE MUSIC. Her characterization of the Queen was hilarious. Her first entrance was one to remember and to cherish.

The next time that I saw Mary Boland was on a very hot June night at the Cox Theatre in Cincinnati. This was a summer stock performance in a revival of one of her greatest hits, MEET THE WIFE. Even with a very mediocre supporting cast she was a riot. I recall so well the lack of air-conditioning, and that we were a large group in Row "B", and that we all nearly fell out of our seats with laughter. There was one moment involving a telephone call which was priceless.

I saw Miss Boland for the last time in a revival of THE RIVALS at the Taft Theatre in Cincinnati. I had been quite thrilled when I read that this revival was coming to town, as it was an all star cast including Bobby Clark, Walter Hampden, and others. I felt that the role of Mrs. Malaprop would be just perfect for Miss Boland. I had not seen the play since I saw it with Mrs. Fiske some fifteen hears before. However, I was greatly disappointed. Somehow, while she was very funny at times, she never really seemed to be right for this foolish woman who has become a classic character in Restoration Comedy. Perhaps she was tired and not at her best, but somehow she left a feeling that much more could have been done to make Mrs. Malaprop come alive. I also recall that she had costumed it very badly, and that the frills and furbelows seemed out of place. I am sorry that this was the last time that I saw her on the stage.

Of course, I saw her many times in the films. I best recall her in RUGGLES OF RED GAP, in which she was at her very best. The cast included Charlie Ruggles and Charles Laughton. I also remember her in PRIDE AND PREJUDICE. She was excellent as Mrs. Bennett. Greer Garson and Laurence Olivier were in the cast, also.

Yes, we shall miss Miss Boland very much. Her talent was unique.

ALICE BRADY

My memories of Alice Brady fall into the same category as those of John Barrymore. This is because, unfortunately, I did not see her in her two greatest roles. From reports of friends who did see these plays, I realize now how much I must have missed. The roles were: Ina Bowman, in BRIDE OF THE LAMB, and Lavinia, in MOURNING BECOMES ELECTRA.

I saw Miss Brady for the first time at the Empire Theatre in New York, on 23 August, 1923, as Mamie in ZANDER THE GREAT. This play gave ample evidence of the great personal charm of Miss Brady, and the melodramatic plot was entertaining, if not great. It proved to me, also, that she really was an outstanding actress. I, of course, had seen her many times in the films, and I was happy to see her on the stage. Her supporting cast was interesting: Jerome Patrick as the cowboy, Dan, and George Abbott as Texas.

The following spring, when she was on tour, I saw this play again, on 18 April, 1924, at the Majestic Theatre in Peoria. I enjoyed it all over again. There were cast changes, but interesting ones. Victor Sutherland was the Dan, and Charles Bickford was the Texas. In the two times that I saw the play, the Zander was James Dunn.

Miss Brady's untimely death, on 28 October, 1939, at the age of 47, was a great loss to the American theatre. She was a vibrant and exciting actress.

LILLIAN BRAITHWAITE

Lillian Braithwaite has long been one of the most famous actresses on the London stage. She had a great dignity, a great sense of the theatre, and she was an actress who demanded attention.

I saw her only once, and this was late in her career. The date was in July, 1936, at the Criterion Theatre in London. The play was THE LADY OF LA PAZ. It was a drama about a woman who was seeking to live down her past, and who was trying to live again and to forget, at least for the moment, all of her indiscretions of other years. It was also important as a stage piece to bring Miss Braithwaite once again before her London public. In the cast was the young Nova Pilbeam who had just recently, as of the season 1935-1936, made quite a name for herself in the films. They played together very well, even with their wide differences in stage experience: the young actress who was making her stage debut, and the seasoned actress who had had years of experience.

The play was inconsequential, but the setting in La Paz, Bolivia, was very authentic and very beautiful, as I recall. Miss Braithwaite rose to the occasion when the script gave her a chance, and she gave definite proof of the very fine actress that she was. I was very pleased that I had been able to see her at least once, as I had read of her many great performances through the years.

FANNIE BRICE

I first saw Fannie Brice in the ZIEGFIELD FOLLIES OF 1919 on New Year's Eve, 1919, at the Colonial Theatre in Chicago. Three moments come back to me in my memory. First was her singing of "Second Hand Rose", with all of the verve of the early ragtime songs; it was catchy and full of rhythm. Second, there was a skit, a burlesque of CAMILLE, which she played with W. C. Fields and Raymond Hitchcock; it was a complete riot and I have never forgotten her "emoting" and the delicious satire. Third was in the second half of the show when she sang "My Man" leaning against a lamp post; this memory is a cherished one. This was perhaps the most famous moment of her career, and the one that everyone remembers, if they were fortunate enough to have heard her sing it. It is a haunting song, and no one else has been able to sing it in quite the same way, with its pathos and its simplicity.

It was fifteen years before I saw Miss Brice again. This was in the ZIEGFIELD FOLLIES OF 1934. It was in November of 1934 that I saw it at the Shubert Theatre in Cincinnati. This was after Mr. Ziegfield's death, and the show was produced by Billie Burke. It was a far cry from the other FOLLIES, but it did have its moments. Two songs come back: "Soul Saving Sadie" and "Sarah the Sunshine Girl". Then, too, it included the skit of "Baby Snooks" which she had done for several years over the radio. This was perhaps the highlight of the show. It also included a very funny ballet scene with Miss Brice as a ballerina. From my own standpoint, this was the hit of the show. Miss Brice was a great comedienne and she possessed great personal appeal.

BILLIE BURKE

Billie Burke brings back so many memories. She, too, was a great favorite in the silent movie days. How could anyone ever forget GLORIA'S ROMANCE? Each week this serial came upon the screen and we all waited avidly for the next installment. She has had a long and interesting career. She had many years on the stage before she went into the films, so she has always been an accomplished actress with a great following. In the midst of all of this fame she decided to return to the stage which was, after all, her greatest thrill.

I first saw Billie Burke "in person" during the season of 1922, at the Powers Theatre in Chicago. The play was THE INTIMATE STRANGERS written by Booth Tarkington. It was a delightful play and Miss Burke was at her best. She had a great cast with her, which included Alfred Lunt, Glenn Hunter, and Elizabeth Patterson.

She then had another period in which she spent a long while in Hollywood, appearing in a wide series of films. She did not return to the stage for several years. I saw her next on 29 December, 1930, at the Ethel Barrymore Theatre in New York. The play was THE TRUTH GAME, a new play written by Ivor Novello who also appeared in it as her leading man. Phoebe Foster was also in the cast. It was an amusing piece written for her special talents, and it enjoyed a long run. She then took another Hollywood sabbatical and appeared in a long series of films, many of them co-starred with Will Rogers.

Fourteen years went by before I saw her again. This was on 6 May, 1944, at the Belasco Theatre in New York. The play was MRS. JANUARY AND MR. X in which she was co-starred with Frank Craven. Time had been kind to her and she gave an enchanting performance in a rather dull play. Also in the cast was Barbara Bel Geddes, and she radiated youth and wholesomeness. There were certain moments, even in this play, in which the old quality of "special beauty and grace" came over the footlights. It was a pleasure to see her once more, and I wouldn't have missed it for anything.

Of all of the films, those with Will Rogers stand out, and so do DINNER AT EIGHT and A BILL OF DIVORCEMENT. In all of these she seemed to radiate the quality that had made her famous for so many years.

Miss Burke died at the age of 85 in 1970 in California.

DAVID BURNS

The death of David Burns this past March, 1971, while he was playing at the Forrest Theatre in Philadelphia, was a tremendous shock to the entire profession. This was true, also, for the large number of admirers of his gifted talent.

Frequently one is apt to use the words "a great actor" without thinking very clearly. Actually, there are very few really great actors. Mr. Burns was certainly one of this small number.

My first chance to see him brings back many happy memories. I had read, of course, of the fabulous success in New York of OKLAHOMA. No tickets were available for many months. So, when it was announced that the National Company was to open at the National Theatre in Washington on 18 October, 1943, I sent in a mail order, and was rewarded by being able to see the second performance on Tuesday, 19 October, 1943.

The wonders of this beautiful musical were well worth the long wait. In this way I was first introduced to David Burns. He was playing the role of Ali Hakim, and gave a very amusing and utterly engaging performance. His big number, "It's a scandal, it's an outrage" brought down the house, and he had to repeat the number. The entire production was as nearly perfect as a show can be. The Theatre Guild had chosen very wisely in the second cast, and it was the equal in every way to the original one in New York. Harry Stockwell, known throughout the world as the "voice" in that very popular and enjoyable film, SNOW WHITE AND THE SEVEN DWARVES was the Curly. Evelyn Wyckoff was the Laurey and Pamela Britton was the Ado Annie. They were all excellent.

Mr. Burns for many months played the role of Vandergelder with Carol Channing in HELLO, DOLLY, but he was not in the cast when I saw the show. My loss.

From the musical comedy actor to the role that he played in Arthur Miller's outstanding play, THE PRICE, is a very great accomplishment. However, he made the transition with great ease. In the pre-Broadway tour of this play I saw him as Gregory Solomon in January, 1968, at the Walnut Street Theatre in Philadelphia. Mr. Solomon has come to appraise the antiques which are in the home of the Franz family. The parents are now dead and the two brothers who have had no contact with each other for many years have come to close the home. Mr. Burns gave a performance of quiet humility that will rank with some of the greatest performances I have ever seen on the stage. His interpretation was a joy to watch as it unfolded. Pat Hingle as the policeman brother, and Arthur Kennedy as the lawyer were both excellent. Kate Reid again gave one of her telling performances as the wife of the policeman. It was great theatre.

I saw Mr. Burns for the last time on the opening night of 70 GIRLS 70 at the Forrest Theatre in Philadelphia. The date was in March, 1971. In this nostalgic musical, David Burns was co-starred with Mildred Natwick. Enough to say that he was back in a musical, and he gave it all that he had and much more. His two big numbers were "The Caper" in Act One, and "Go Visit" in Act Two. In the latter he appeared with the young lad who was the only one in the cast who wasn't past sixty. Both numbers were show-stoppers. He was, as always, winning and charming. In a way, it is wonderful for an old trouper to die while in harness--but we shall miss him.

SPRING BYINGTON

This charming and gracious actress has been too long missing from our theatre. Granted, not too long ago, we could always turn on the T. V. and see her in DECEMBER BRIDE, a series in which she delighted thousands, over a period of years. I always marvelled at her constant ability to play the roles that she did with, seemingly, so little effort. She was very pretty and very feminine. (She still is). I saw her only twice on the stage, and each time she left a very definite impression upon my memory.

I saw her first on 7 September, 1924, when she was playing at the Adelphi Theatre in Chicago. The play was BEGGAR ON HORSEBACK with Roland Young and Osgood Perkins. Here she was Mrs. Caddy and this began a long series of very funny characterizations in which she was one of the brightest additions to any cast she happened to be in. In this sense she was never really a "star" in the sense that word connotates through the years; but her presence was always known, and she managed by her wit, charm, and good humor to win over any audience.

The only other time that I saw Spring Byington was during Christmas week of 1932, eight years later, at the Royale Theatre in New York. The play was WHEN LADIES MEET. In this very amusing play she played the role of Bridgit. It was played with great understanding, and even with a touch of pathos. Frieda Inescort and Selena Royal were also in the cast. It was a most pleasant theatrical experience.

Her film appearances were many and I saw them whenever I could, but I still relish the good fortune I had in seeing her on the stage, at least twice. I do wish that she would come back, at least once more.

Miss Byington died on 8 September, 1971 in California. She was 84.

LOUIS CALHERN

Mr. Calhern was a very popular leading man who possessed a good deal of talent. In his later years, he became a star in his own right.

I saw him first on 29 November, 1929, at the Harris Theatre in Chicago. He was playing with Ethel Barrymore in THE LOVE DUEL. He played the role of He. He was suave and sophisticated in a part that was tailored to his talents.

I saw him again the following year on 17 and 21 February, 1930 at the Shubert Theatre in Cincinnati when he was on tour with Miss Barrymore. Now he was in both THE KINGDOM OF GOD and THE LOVE DUEL. In the former, he appeared only in the second act as Errique, the persistent suitor who tried to keep the "Sister" from taking her final vows to become a nun. Again he had the same quality of urbanity and worldly wisdom.

The last time that I saw Mr. Calhern was seventeen years later, on 27 February, 1947. This was at the Cox Theatre in Cincinnati, and by now he was a very fine character actor, and a star. The play was THE MAGNIFICENT YANKEE. As Mr. Justice Holmes, he was no longer the matinee idol, and he created a really superior character. The wisdom, the humor, and the dignity that the role demanded fitted him perfectly. It was a memorable performance, filled with human compassion. Sylvia Field was a touching and gracious Mrs. Holmes.

Mr. Calhern died in 1968.

EDDIE CANTOR

This comedian has long been one of our most popular and admired entertainers. His career has covered many years and in every field: the legitimate theatre, films, night clubs, and T. V.

Although I only saw him once, that memory has stayed with me as a most pleasing and enjoyable experience. The one time was on 4 November, 1925, at the Woods Theatre in Chicago. The musical was KID BOOTS, in which he was ably supported by Mary Eaton and Jobyanna Howland.

As I write this sketch, over forty years later, I find that I recall very little of the plot; but I do remember with amusement Mr. Cantor, as he danced across the stage singing, "If You Knew Susie, Like I Knew Susie", and other tunes. He was a small man and his big wide eyes behind the glasses gave him a "Pucklike" expression, even though he was certainly more knowing than that famous character of Shakespeare.

Besides being a great entertainer, he was a very fine man who gave of himself to aid many others in his profession who were less fortunate than he.

RUTH CHATTERTON

There was always a feeling about Ruth Chatterton that she was a "lady to the manor born". She had a warm personality and a quiet manner; her voice was low and pleasing. My memories of Miss Chatterton begin when she was a young actress. Since I saw her but twice, and a period of over twenty-five years intervened, it is a little hard for me to evaluate her as an actress.

I saw her first on 31 March, 1921, at the Majestic Theatre in Peoria. The play was J. M. Barrie's MARY ROSE. In this play I do recall that she had all of the qualities that the role demanded. These included the somewhat ethereal wistfulness of the young girl who had been lost to the outside world for so many years, but somehow had never seemed to change, and a certain joy of living that was very engaging. There was, also, a haunting quality about the entire play. Tom Nesbitt was her leading man.

Twenty-six years later I saw her again, in a summer stock performance in July of 1947. The place was in Olney, Maryland. The play was Lillian Hellman's THE LITTLE FOXES. The years had been kind to Miss Chatterton, and she was as lovely and elusive as ever. However, she was woefully miscast as Regina Giddons. The role demands the hardness, the selfishness, the calculating qualities of a very clever women. Miss Chatterton did not rise to these, and the performance lacked balance. She was much too nice a person, and one could never really feel that she could have schemed and planned the complete downfall of her whole family pattern. I was glad to see her once more, but I have always wished that it could have been in another play.

When I read of her death in 1968, I was saddened, and I regretted not having seen her in some of her more famous roles.

MADY CHRISTIANS

With a long and varied career in the European theatre in Vienna and Berlin, Miss Christians came to America more or less as an unknown actress. She soon mastered the language difficulties, and in a few years she became one of our most accomplished actresses. She was tremendously versatile playing the great roles, such as Gertrude in HAMLET, as well as becoming a fine comedienne.

I saw her first on 2 April, 1942, at the Taft Theatre in Cincinnati. The play was THE WATCH ON THE RHINE, Lillian Hellman's brilliant play about the effect of the Second World War upon the ordinary people who were caught in its web quite accidentally but who had the stamina to rebel. Mady Christians played the wife of a refugee and she was poignant, as with her new found strength she coped with the problem which confronted her. Lucille Watson, a very great character actress, and Paul Lucas, who was just coming into his own on the American stage, were also in the cast. It was very fine theatre.

I saw her next in what was perhaps her most memorable role: Mama in I REMEMBER MAMA. This was on 17 February, 1945, at the Music Box Theatre in New York. This heartwarming play, which John Van Druten had written from a series of short stories, brought out all of the sensitive, sincere qualities of Miss Christians' acting. She _was_ Mama. I shall long remember her performance as one of the real highlights of my many years of playgoing. Her supporting cast was equally fine. It included Oscar Holmoka as Uncle Chris, and the talented Joan Tetzel and Marlon Brando as two of her children.

The last time I saw Miss Christians was at the end of August in 1949. She was touring in summer stock this summer, and I was fortunate to see her at the Chevy Chase Summer Theatre outside of Chicago. The play was THE VINEGAR TREE. I had seen it many years before with Mary Boland, but I was happy to see it again. In this play Miss Christians was at her best as a full-fledged comedienne. It is a frothy play, but it has undercurrents of seriousness which make good comedy.

In the preceding spring of 1949, Miss Christians came to Cincinnati to give a lecture at the Cincinnati Women's Club. This was for members only, but because of my interest in the theatre and my long years of experience as a director, I was able to wangle an invitation. After her very clever and amusing lecture on her experiences in the theatre, I was introduced to her at the tea which followed. She was witty and vivacious and very much the actress. It was a pleasant experience. The last years of her career were fraught with sorrow and complete misunderstanding as she was falsely accused of collaboration with a subversive group. She was finally cleared, but it broke her spirit and she died on 28 October, 1951, in New York. Her death was a tragic waste of a great talent in our theatre.

INA CLAIRE

Ina Claire is one of the most luminous actresses in our theatre. She has a certain quality of grace, and an abundance of charm and personality. During the many years of her varied career, she has come to be one of our most popular stars. In the early years she was in musical comedy, and after a long period of careful training she mastered the art of the comedienne.

The first time that I saw Miss Claire was during this transition period. She was in vaudeville in a dramatic skit entitled RIGHT YOU ARE. I picked this up at the Palace Theatre in Chicago, during the season of 1922. She was ably supported by Geoffrey Kerr.

By the next time that I saw her, she had become a full-fledged actress, and she was rapidly gaining the fame and glory which she has had for over thirty-five years. The play was THE LAST OF MRS. CHEYNEY, a delightful comedy by Frederick Lonsdale. Her performance as Mrs. Cheyney was one of the delights of that particular season. The date was during the season of 1927, at the Blackstone Theatre in Chicago. Her leading man was Roland Young. He gave her excellent support and their scenes together were a delight.

I saw her next in one of her most popular and famous plays, BIOGRAPHY. I saw it first at the Avon Theatre in New York, on 20 March, 1933. Her leading men were Earle Larrimore and Jay Fasset. The play is listed as one of the ten best plays of that year, and it gave Ina Claire one of her best roles. I saw BIOGRAPHY again on 2 November, 1933, while it was on tour, at the Shubert Theatre in Cincinnati. She had lost none of her ability to give the role her best, and it was good to see it again. Jay

Fassett was still in the cast, but Larrimore had been replaced by Shepherd Strudwick who was also very fine in the part.

I saw her next at the Cox Theatre in Cincinnati, in November of 1936, when she was on tour with END OF SUMMER. The original cast were with her this time, including Osgood Perkins and Van Hefflin. This is one of Mr. Behrman's best plays--a satire on the idle rich and the problems that they might have to face in the event that our government becomes socialistic. Miss Claire's wide-eyed wonder at this prospect, and her final line given to Mr. Hefflin, "Come the revolution, I'll have a friend in high office," has somehow remained with me through the years.

The last time that I saw Ina Claire was again at the Cox Theatre in Cincinnati, the date, 6 October, 1947. In the eleven years she had lost none of her special appeal. The play was THE FATAL WEAKNESS by George Kelly. In this she played a divorcee who could neither help nor change her weakness for attending weddings. In this case it was her ex-husband's re-marriage. It was a delightful performance and I shall long remember her final scene when she is all dressed to leave, and she turns for a bit of encouragement from her oldest friend, and then leaves the stage.

She has returned to New York at least once since that time, when she appeared in a T. S. Elliot play there, but I was unable to be in New York at that time. She now lives in retirement with her husband in San Francisco.

GEORGE M. COHAN

My enjoyment of the "Great Song and Dance Man" was limited to his straight plays until the last time that I saw him.

I first saw Mr. Cohan on 18 December, 1930, at the Grand Opera House in Cincinnati. The play was THE TAVERN. He had played in this famous old show many times in his career, and it was now on its last revival. The fun of this old comedy-melodrama lies in its improbability, and its example of old school acting. It was still intact, and in spite of a very mediocre supporting cast, Mr. Cohan was very engaging.

I next saw him in July, 1933 at the Harris Theatre in Chicago. The play was PIGEONS AND PEOPLE. This was a comic "stunt" play which proved to be no more than a lark. "A comic state of mind in one act without an intermission" is stated in the program. It was pure Cohan surrounded by a bevy of girls, and it was an amusing evening.

My memories of George M. Cohan as a really fine actor came with his performance in Eugene O'Neill's AH, WILDERNESS. I saw it first on 29 March, 1934, at the Guild Theatre in New York. The play was a touching reminder of youth and all of its problems. Cohan's performance as the father was human and creative. It was a remarkable change from his own plays, in which he had appeared for so long, and he gave it his best. It was a very rewarding experience. I saw it again on tour on 21 February, 1935, at the Shubert Theatre in Cincinnati. It was still a most charming evening in the theatre. Elisha Cook, Jr. played the son in both performances. He had great feeling and understanding of the disturbed adolescent.

I finally saw Mr. Cohan as the "Song and Dance Man" in the fall of 1938, at the Auditorium Theatre in Chicago. The musical was I'D RATHER

BE RIGHT. It proved to be a somewhat contrived piece on the peculiarities of President F. D. R. It was a huge "spoof" with a mediocre musical score, and very little to recommend it save a bravura performance by Cohan. He was no longer young, but he gave the show a feeling of youth and vitality. His dancing was a sensation, and this alone made it worth while. I am glad that I saw him in both fields of endeavor. He was a tremendous showman, whose death in New York on 5 November, 1942, closed an era of unique American showmanship.

CONSTANCE COLLIER

Miss Collier had been a famous actress both in London and in New York before I was able to see her. She was a very great actress, and will rank with the very best.

I saw her only once, in June 1933, at the Grand Opera House in Chicago. The play was DINNER AT EIGHT. As Carlotta Vance, an actress of another era, she was outstanding. Her dignity of manner, her poise and sureness of touch, and her beautiful speaking voice, were all still at their best. She gave the role real purpose, and most definitely she was the star of the large cast of very able actors who were also in the play. The play was interesting because it gave a panorama of a certain type of American life. A large dinner party served as the focal point for learning of the inner lives of this special group of people. Will one ever forget her speech which begins: "May I take you for a stroll down Forty-second Street and a little look at the Carlotta Vance Theatre? For the past six months they haven't taken the lock off the door." etc. The cast was impressive: Ann Andrews as the hostess, Jane Wyatt as the disturbed daughter, and Crane Wilbur as the actor who had seen better days. Sam Levene was also in the cast as was Mary Murray, in a small part. This is only important to me because she was a neighbor in my early youth and had gone to New York to get into the theatre; she succeeded, but only in small roles. It was a treat to see her, and I was very excited to know someone in this huge cast.

As far as I know this was one of Miss Collier's last performances. She spent the last years of her life as a teacher of dramatics. She was a very valuable asset to the younger actors and actresses, because she knew all of the best ways to achieve perfect diction. A few years later, I read that she had died in California.

PATRICIA COLLINGE

What fond and wonderful memories I have of Patricia Collinge! Today she is in retirement, and we only hear from her through the clever short stories that she writes, every now and then, in THE NEW YORKER magazine. But my good fortune in seeing her as a very fine and an accomplished actress covers a period of over thirty years.

I first saw Miss Collinge when she was a very young actress, not long out of her native Ireland. I, too, was only fourteen at that time. The date was the season of 1917-1918, and the theatre was the Majestic in Peoria. She was playing in POLLYANNA. Her leading man was a young Philip Merrivale who was making an early appearance in the United States, also. The play was a dramatization of the ever popular novel of Eleanor Porter, and it had a wide appeal. As a child, I recall that I adored it.

I saw her next, a year or so later, on the 25th of October, 1919, again at the Majestic Theatre in Peoria. The play this time was TILLIE, taken from the popular stories, TILLIE, THE MENNONITE MAID. Here again she charmed her audience with this simple tale. (I note in my program that also in the cast was a young Elliott Nugent.)

By the next time that I saw her she had really become a seasoned actress, and gave sure evidence of the great actress that she became later. This was during the season of 1923-1924, at the Blackstone Theatre in Chicago. The play was JUST SUPPOSE, that charming bit of romantic nonsense in which she played a southern belle bewitched in the magnolia gardens by the possibility that the strange guest that night might be the Prince of Wales. It was a very delightful performance. She was supported by Leslie Howard, Geoffrey Kerr and Elizabeth Patterson.

I saw her next, again in Chicago, at the Playhouse Theatre. The date was 25 August, 1925; the play, TARNISH. Her leading man was Frederic March. She was playing now a much more mature and serious role, and this helped to show her great versatility.

The next time that I saw her was on 12 September, 1932, again in Chicago, but this time at the Harris Theatre. The play was ANOTHER LANGUAGE. Her leading man this time was Tom Powers. The warmth and understanding that she gave to this role was a joy to behold.

Seven years later, on 19 June, 1939, at the National Theatre in New York, I saw her give her finest performance. She was playing the role of Birdie in the performance of THE LITTLE FOXES starring Tallulah Bankhead and Frank Conroy. Patricia Collinge's characterization of the pathetic Birdie will long remain in my memory as one of the greatest performances I have ever seen.

Ten more years went by before I saw her again, unhappily, for the last time. The play was THE HEIRESS, which starred Basil Rathbone and Beatrice Straight. However, Miss Collinge gave a very fine performance of the aunt who befriended the daughter. It was good to see her again.

She has never lost her Irish charm, and she will always remain one of my favorite actresses.

FAYE COMPTON

Faye Compton had a long and varied career on the London stage, and infrequent appearances in New York before I saw her.

I saw her only once, and this was in July, 1936, at the Globe Theatre in London. The play was CALL IT A DAY by Dodie Smith. This is by far Miss Smith's best play. Faye Compton played the wife. She was excellent in the role, and she had the creative ability that so many of the British actresses seem to acquire through the years. The comedy was very English in its setting, and in its acting; however, its theme was universal. There are days in every home in which the entire structure of the family pattern can easily be broken, or at least woefully bent if the wrong turn or the wrong decision is followed. On the surface the play might seem to be exaggerated; but, in thinking it over, one can easily see that it could happen anywhere. It was beautifully mounted and artistically acted by a wonderful cast which included: Owen Nares, Marie Lohr, and Patricia Hilliard, a young and promising film star of that day.

I enjoyed seeing Miss Compton very much, and I have always wished that I might have seen her again.

GLADYS COOPER

Miss Cooper has a great talent. She is able to play any number of roles from serious drama to high comedy. She has been on the stage for many years, and she has appeared in several plays in New York. Unfortunately, I was never in New York when she was. However, I have followed her career during these years. (Also, I have been fascinated by the astonishingly beautiful picture which appears in the bound volume of the old Vanity Fair magazine taken at the time when she was most famous.)

So, it was with great pleasure that I finally saw Gladys Cooper in May, 1970, at the St. Martin's Theatre in London. The play was OUT OF THE QUESTION. She was again playing comedy. While the play was by no means a great play, it did have its moments, and Miss Cooper was having a wonderful time. Although she was now in her eighties, she had ease of movement, great comedy sense, tremendous charm, and there were still many traces of her great beauty.

I was fortunate to see her again in May, 1971, at the Haymarket Theatre in London. This time she was in a revival of THE CHALK GARDEN. This is a far better play and it gave her a chance to show her varied talents. In this she was playing Mrs. St. Maugham, a role that she had played before in both London and New York. She played it brilliantly, with all of the subtle undertones that the role requires. She was costumed in excellent taste, and she looked lovely. Joan Greenwood was the Miss Madrigal, and she, too gave a thrilling performance.

It is ironic that I saw Miss Cooper on her last performance in the theatre even as I had seen Marie Tempest in her last performance (in 1939). Miss Cooper died in November, 1971, in her home outside London, at the age of eighty-two.

KATHARINE CORNELL

My memories of Katharine Cornell cover a period of over forty years. During this time I have always been inspired and thrilled with her great talent, her beauty, and her warm understanding. She is one of our really great actresses and in each role that she plays she gives a rare and wonderful gift of gracious humility. While she speaks rapidly, she has a melodious voice, and she is always articulate.

I saw Katharine Cornell for the first time on 26 April, 1925, at the Selwyn Theatre in Chicago. She was playing in the pre-Broadway tryouts of THE GREEN HAT. The play, taken from Michael Arlen's best seller of the day was pure, sentimental melodrama, not a very good play but a very popular one. Her performance as Iris March was effective and appealing. She was supported by Leslie Howard and Ann Harding.

I saw her next four years later, on 25 November, 1929, again at the Selwyn Theatre in Chicago. The play was THE AGE OF INNOCENCE. Again, this was a dramatization of a well-known novel, this one by Edith Wharton. In every way it was a much better play, and her understanding of the role of Countess Olenska made it a very moving performance. Arnold Korff and John Marsden were her leading men.

On 6 July, 1931, I saw her at the Empire Theatre in New York, as Elizabeth Barrett in THE BARRETTS OF WIMPOLE STREET. I suppose that this is her best known and her most memorable role. She received great acclaim and I was thrilled with the entire performance; it has long remained one of my favorites. Brian Ahern, Margalo Gillmore, and Charles Waldron were in her cast.

I saw Miss Cornell next at the Harris Theatre in Chicago, on 5 June, 1933. The play was ALIEN CORN. This was a very fine play, and one in which she was at her very best. The smoldering frustration of the young girl caught in the web of a small Iowa college town was a masterful example of dramatic technique. She had a brilliant supporting cast which included Lily Cahill, James Rennie, and Luther Adler.

During the next season she went on her long tour of the United States and Canada, with three great plays in her repertoire. She stopped by for the week 2-7 April, 1934, at the Shubert Theatre in Cincinnati, and I was able to see all three. THE BARRETTS was the first in the bill, and it was as sensitively played as ever. There were cast changes, notably Basil Rathbone for Brian Ahern, and while he had his moments, he could in no way compare with Mr. Ahern's Browning. I am sure that I was not alone in waiting for the chance to see Miss Cornell's Juliet. I was in no way disappointed. Every moment, from her first entrance at the masqued ball when she meets Romeo for the first time, until the final tragic scene in the tomb, she was at her superlative best. She was always in complete mastery of the role. Her Juliet, to my mind, was the finest that I have ever seen, and I have seen a goodly number over the years. She was young, she was passionate, she was in love; she was frightened in the potion scene. It was a real landmark in her long and great career. Basil Rathbone read the lines beautifully, but he was not the romantic Romeo that one hopes for. Nor was the young Orson Welles ready for Mercutio. Bertha Belmore as the nurse had moments, but they were fleeting. While Miss Cornell had played CANDIDA many times, I had never had a chance to see her before in this famous Shaw play. She brought all of her warmth and quiet humor to the role, and it was a beautiful performance. Orson Welles fitted the part of Marchbanks far better than he had Mercutio in

ROMEO AND JULIET. Basil Rathbone's Morrell was cold and humorless. All in all, it was a great week in the theatre.

Two years later I saw Miss Cornell again, this time at the Cox Theatre in Cincinnati. The date was 7 December, 1936. The play was Maxwell Anderson's THE WINGLESS VICTORY. As the half-caste native from the south seas brought into the closed society of Salem, Massachusetts, during the year 1800, she was moving, pathetic, and very appealing. This was the first of several pre-Broadway tours that she brought out on the road. She had a fine supporting cast: Myron McCormick, Effie Shannon, and Walter Abel.

I saw her next in April of 1939, at the Taft Theatre in Cincinnati. The play was NO TIME FOR COMEDY. This was the first time that she had appeared in a purely comedy role, and she mastered this medium with ease. It was also a pre-Broadway performance. As her leading man she had Laurence Olivier, who was just coming into prominence in the United States. They played together with great understanding and gave to this somewhat vague comedy a sense of substance. Margalo Gillmore was also in the cast. It was an amusing comedy of manners which went on to great success.

The next time that she came to our town was two years later, in February, 1941, again at the Cox Theatre in Cincinnati. This was in the almost perfect revival of Shaw's THE DOCTOR'S DILEMMA. It was so beautifully staged and so magnificently acted that it was a complete joy from beginning to end. Her Jennifer was all wisdom and humility. She had a brilliant cast with her which included: Raymond Massey, Bramwell Fletcher, Clarence Derwent, and Colin Keith-Johnson. It was a rare treat in the theatre.

Just a year later, on 26 February, 1942, again at the Cox Theatre in Cincinnati, she tried out ROSE BURKE. This was one of the very few errors in judgment that she and her husband, Guthrie McClintic ever made. It was a translation of a French play which was a period melodrama of the old school of the theatre. It was dated, it was on the whole very uninteresting as a play, and in some ways it was downright embarrassing. In spite of a cast of seasoned actors it failed. Philip Merivale was woefully miscast and seemed very ill at ease. Jean Pierre Aumont was making his American debut; he was engaging, but little else. Only the pleasure of seeing Catherine Calhoun Doucet again made the evening even amusing.

With this failure behind her Miss Cornell turned to Chekov. Her revival of THE THREE SISTERS erased all of the misjudgment of the year before. It was a beautiful production in every way. She again surrounded herself with an all-star cast and she played a secondary role of Masha. I saw it on opening night, 30 November, 1942, at the National Theatre in Washington, D. C. Judith Anderson was the Olga, and Gertrude Musgrove was the Irina. Other roles were played by Alexander Knox, Edmund Gwynne, Dennis King, Tom Powers, and Ruth Gordon.

I saw Miss Cornell next in a modern play, LOVERS AND FRIENDS, written by Dodie Smith, on 12 February, 1944, at the Plymouth Theatre in New York. Her leading man was again Raymond Massey. The play was not a great one, but it had certain appeal. It was a war play and it was timely. It went back over a decade to the first World War and it showed the change in morals and the effect of war on quite ordinary people.

Two years later, after the Second World War, I saw her in ANTIGONE on 21 January, 1946, at the Cox Theatre in Cincinnati. This was a revival, in modern dress, of this ageless tragedy. It was done with no sets and was unique in many ways. Its timeless theme was brought up to date to parallel experiences in our present century. While it was effective theatre, and exciting, it lacked the grandeur of the original. Sir Cedric Hardwicke was the Creon.

For a long while Miss Cornell had been promising her wide and enthusiastic public that she would do ANTONY AND CLEOPATRA. When this finally came into reality everyone was awaiting this challenge with eager anticipation. I was fortunate in seeing it twice. First, at the beginning of its run, during its tryout period, and the second time at the end of its career after it had been in New York. There was a very definite growth in her characterization of the complex character of Cleopatra between the two performances. I saw it first on 27 October, 1947 at the Emery Auditorium in Cincinnati. The production was opulent and had the grandeur of ancient Egypt, it was exciting, and it was beautifully played by the entire cast. Outstanding performances were given by Godfrey Tearle as Antony, Kent Smith as Enobarbas, and Lenore Ulric as Charmaine. While Miss Cornell was a better Cleopatra than any that I had ever seen, she was still "feeling out" the greatness of the role. Her beautiful voice was a joy to hear in the verse of Shakespeare. Her physical beauty was perfect for the role, but it was still very static and incomplete--the "infinite variety" seemed to be lacking. I saw it again on 29 March, 1948, at Fords' Theatre in Baltimore, and by now all of the uneveness of the first performance was gone. She was now the regal queen of the Nile. She was the epitome of passion and desire, and she was breathtakingly tragic in her final scene. It was one of her greatest achievements.

Two years later I saw her on 10 April, 1950, at the Hartman Theatre in Columbus. The play was THAT LADY, a romantic drama of Spanish intrigue in Madrid set in the sixteenth century. It was a strange play, and in some ways not very well written, but it had its moments of high drama and excitement. Miss Cornell as the Princess Eboli was shrewd and masterful wearing a black patch over one eye. Her supporting cast included: Henry Daniell, Torin Thatcher, and Henry Stephenson.

The next time that I saw her was a little over a year later, on 17 November, 1951, again at the Hartman Theatre in Columbus. She had decided to revive Somerset Maugham's THE CONSTANT WIFE, which I had seen thirty years before with Ethel Barrymore, and I was most interested in this revival. It was also a pre-Broadway performance. It had been a long time since Miss Cornell had chosen to play comedy, and this also made the revival a matter of importance. Her talent did not fail her, and while her Constance, the wife, was played in a somewhat heavier vein than the one played by Miss Barrymore, she was charming and winning and very feminine in the role. With her she had Grace George, playing her final performances in our theatre, as the mother. In her usual gracious manner Miss Cornell built up the part of the mother, and she gave every possible moment to Miss George. Brian Ahern played the confused husband and John Emery played Bernard Kersal.

Four years later I saw Miss Cornell for the last time. This was on 2 January, 1955, at the Taft Theatre in Cincinnati. This was another pre-Broadway performance. The play was THE DARK IS LIGHT ENOUGH. This was a very confusing play which was beautifully staged and acted, but it left much to be desired in clear continuity. It seemed to ramble on and on and really reach no conclusion. Tyrone Power, Jr., and Christopher Plummer were in her cast.

It seems incredible that now, as I write these memoirs of the theatre, that I have not seen Katharine Cornell for over fifteen years. She has been in several plays in New York but they have never toured. With Brian Ahern she played for two seasons in DEAR LIAR, traveling up and down the entire country, but for some unexplainable reason she never brought it to Cincinnati. This was our loss.

I miss seeing her very much, and I only hope that she finds one more good play before she retires from the theatre altogether.

JANE COWL

My memories of Jane Cowl cover a span of twenty-eight years. She was always my mother's favorite actress, and her beauty and great talent were shown to me at a very early age. For a year we had been living in the wilds of Minnesota, where my father had a large dairy farm to sell. It had been a dull winter with no theatre. If this sounds overly precocious for a child of fourteen I am sorry, but I can't help it. Spring finally came, and the thrill of moving back home was uppermost in our minds. Watching the Minneapolis newspapers--the city seemed a million miles away, but it was only about one hundred--we noted that we would miss LILAC TIME. Mother and I were crushed. Dad had gone home early to find us a new house, but I had to stay on to finish school. Imagine our thrill to discover that Jane Cowl was to come to Peoria, too! So, I finally saw Jane Cowl in LILAC TIME on 30 May, 1918, at the Majestic Theatre. (It is interesting to note that it was a whole year before I saw my adored Ethel Barrymore on the same stage.) Mother was happy to see her favorite actress, I was thrilled to see a famous actress, and both of us relished every moment of seeing *any* play again. I recall the haunting beauty of her voice, and I revelled in the sentimentality of this old war play.

The next time I saw Miss Cowl was at the Cort Theatre in Chicago on 6 November, 1920. The play was SMILIN' THROUGH. This was perhaps one of her most famous roles. The unique quality of this dream play had a great effect upon its audiences. I remember that I loved every moment of it, and I doubtless wept at its very sentimental overtones. When Miss Cowl took it on tour I saw it again at home in Peoria at the Majestic Theatre on 26 January, 1921. I recall that Dad was with us, too it was one of the few times that he was home, since he travelled a great deal in those early days.

It is obvious that Miss Cowl enjoyed playing Peoria, because on 6 October, 1923, she gave us a pre-Broadway glimpse of her Juliet. Her performance in ROMEO AND JULIET with Rollo Peters, Dennis King, and Jessie Ralph has become a legend. Far greater critics than I have stated that it was one of the most beautiful performances of Juliet in our memory. The breath-taking loveliness of the balcony scene is an unforgettable milestone in my theatre experience.

I saw her next on 5 December, 1924 at the Selwyn Theatre in Chicago. (This was, incidentally, my twenty-first birthday). The play was WHO KNOWS. It was a mistake--a very morbid and unhappy play which, if memory serves, did not get much farther than Chicago. Rollo Peters and Jessie Ralph were still with her, but none of them could save a bad play. I recall, too, that that night, to celebrate my birthday, I had a choice between going to see Miss Cowl and going to hear Galli-Curci sing in THE BARBER OF SEVILLE at the Chicago Opera. I have always regretted that I made the wrong choice, for I most certainly could have missed this poor play, even with Jane Cowl.

I did not see her again until 31 March, 1930, at the Cox Theatre in Cincinnati. The play was JENNY. Her leading man was Sir Guy Standing. While it was an amusing trifle, it did little to advance her career except to show what a fine comedienne she could be.

I saw her next in March, 1931, at the Harris Theatre in Chicago. This was in ART AND MRS. BOTTLE. This was a much better comedy and, along with Leon Quartermaine, she managed to give it a great deal of charm and wit. She soon went on tour again, and I saw her do Viola in TWELFTH NIGHT on 20 April, 1931, at the Shubert Theatre in Cincinnati. With a great classical comedy she was at her best. She had just the right feeling for the role, and it was done in a very modern stage set. Leon Quartermaine was the Malvolio, and the ring scene was pure delight.

Five years later, in November of 1936, I saw her in FIRST LADY. This was again at the Cox Theatre in Cincinnati. This is a very funny play, a satire on politics in Washington, D. C. As Lucy Chase Wayne, she gave every evidence of how we might imagine a "First Lady" could be. It was satirical comedy at its best.

The last time that I saw Miss Cowl was ten years later, on 8 July, 1946. It was at the Cox Theatre in Cincinnati. She was touring in summer stock, and she was playing in CANDIDA. While she had many moments of her old charm, and she played the final scene with humor and compassion, the rest of her company were so mediocre that she had little or no support. I have always been sorry that the final time that I thrilled at the husky voice and remembered her great beauty was a somewhat vacant echo of the Jane Cowl whom I had seen first so long ago in 1918. I prefer to remember her as Moonyeen, as Juliet, as Viola and as Lucy Chase Wayne. Miss Cowl had reverses in her last years and was never able to find another really good play. She died in California on 22 June, 1950.

FRANK CRAVEN

The personal charm of Frank Craven was universal. It is interesting that, in going over my scrap books, I recall the first time that I saw him, in 1923, far better than the last time, twenty-one years later, in 1944.

I saw Frank Craven for the first time on 20 January, 1923, at the Woods Theatre in Chicago in a play which he had written, THE FIRST YEAR. I seem to recall every moment of that hilarious comedy--the tragic dinner party, and all of its comic overtones. When he went on tour a few months later, I saw it again on 8 April, 1923, at the Majestic Theatre in Peoria. I laughed all over again. The cast were all excellent, and there were no changes from the Chicago run.

I saw him next on 15 May, 1925, at the Blackstone Theatre in Chicago. The play was NEW BROOMS. Again, he had written the play. It was a simple comedy of American home life, but somehow it wasn't quite as well-written as THE FIRST YEAR. His leading lady was Blythe Daly.

It was fourteen years before I saw him again. This, too, was in Chicago, at the Selwyn Theatre on 30 April, 1939. The play was, of course, OUR TOWN by Thornton Wilder. I suppose that this play, with its universal appeal to all, is one of the finest plays in all American literature. Frank Craven's performance as the Stage Manager was unique. It had all of the New England "twang", and all of the humility of greatness. I recall also that his son, John Craven, was the George, that Martha Scott was Emily, and Evelyn Varden was Mrs. Gibbs. It was a milestone in our theatre.

I saw Frank Craven for the last time on 4 May, 1944, at the Belasco

Theatre in New York. The play was MRS. JANUARY AND MR X, a trifle by Zoe Akins. I was drawn to the theatre to see both Mr. Craven and Billie Burke (with whom he was co-starred), once again. They were both completely charming and a delight to watch, but even they could not breathe life into this bit of nonsense.

Mr. Craven died the next year, on 1 September, 1945.

LAURA HOPE CREWS

I have seen many fine comediennes in our theatre, but Laura Hope Crews has always been my favorite. Her humor always seemed to be so effortless; it was never forced. She was just an adorably funny woman.

I saw Miss Crews for the first time on 5 September, 1919, at the Blackstone Theatre in Chicago. The play was ON THE HIRING LINE. This was a pure comedy of manners. It wasn't a great play, but the many problems of keeping servants on a Long Island estate did make for amusing moments, and Miss Crews carried a magic wand.

I saw her next, not quite a year later, on 6 April, 1920, at the Majestic Theatre in Peoria. The play was TEA FOR THREE which was a much better play. Here the age-old triangle had a new and delightful twist. Her leading men were: Arthur Byron and Frederick Perry. The whole play was a joy to see. However, it was really a forerunner of Noel Coward's DESIGN FOR LIVING which I saw many years later.

It was twenty-two years later before I saw her again. This time it was on 27 February, 1924, at the Cox Theatre in Cincinnati. The play was ARSENIC AND OLD LACE. Her performance of Abby was one of her funniest. Her humor, her timing, and her obvious delight in playing the role were a great lesson in high comedy technique. In her cast were: Effie Shannon, Eric Van Stroheim, and Angie Adams. (Miss Adams is now Mrs. Jack Clark, and has just recently become a relative of mine by marriage.) This was not only the last time that I saw Miss Crews; it was, unfortunately, the last play in which she appeared, for she died the following fall on 13 November, 1942.

Of all of the many films in which I saw her, her Prudence with Garbo in CAMILLE, and her Aunt Pittypat in GONE WITH THE WIND, will always remain in my memory as two of her finest performances.

GWEN FFRANGCON DAVIES

What a wonderful actress! She has had a long and varied career in the London Theatre. She has a mastery of the supreme knowledge of a real theatrical performance. She is very electric in every role that she plays. She does not have regal beauty, but she does have a sense of theatrics that is unique in our modern theatre.

I saw her first in July of 1934, in London at the New Theatre. The play was UEEN OF SCOTS by Gordon Daviott. It was an interesting play about Mary, Queen of Scots, which had been written as a companion piece to the drama written in the United States by Maxwell Anderson, MARY OF SCOTLAND. It was a good play but not quite up to the calibre of Mr. Anderson's play. It did not take Mary to the Tower, and it ended on a much more sympathetic note. Miss Davies was superb in the earlier scenes as the Queen, and she had a regal quality. In the final scene, as a lost and forlorn woman seeking love and understanding, she was pathetic and heart-breaking. Her Bothwell was the young and energetic Laurence Olivier.

It was nearly thirty years before I saw her again. This time it was in her only American appearance, in the all-star cast of the revival of THE SCHOOL FOR SCANDAL in January of 1964, at the Majestic Theatre in New York. For the American performances she had replaced Margaret Rutherford as Mrs. Candor. She was electric and exciting in the role. The years had been kind to her. Also, her supreme knowledge of timing, and her real understanding of the role she was playing, had never changed. It was a challenge to follow the great favorite, Miss Rutherford; but Miss Davies was never at a loss to create the necessary foolishness of the character, Mrs. Candor. Miss Davies is a very remarkable actress, and was definitely "in place" in this timeless classic.

DUDLEY DIGGS

Dudley Diggs was, in my estimation, one of our very finest character actors. It was my misfortune that I never saw him until quite late in his career, but I was fortunate to see him three times.

I saw him first on 24 March, 1937, at the Shubert Theatre in New York. The play was THE MASQUE OF KINGS by Maxwell Anderson. He was playing Franz Joseph, in this story of the Hapsburgs in Vienna in the late 1800's. It was a sure and carefully planned performance. His dignity and restraint were outstanding.

The second time that I saw him was less than a year later, also in New York, at the Guild Theatre, on 27 December, 1937. This time the play was THE GHOST OF YANKEE DOODLE by Sidney Howard. In this play involving appeasement between countries rather than a war, he was playing John Madison Clevenger, a man who was very conservative in his business as well as his private life. He was co-starred with Ethel Barrymore in this, and together they made a fine pair. It was fine, intelligent theatre, but lasted only briefly on Broadway. In the cast, also, was Frank Conroy, a very fine actor.

The third and last time that I saw Mr. Diggs was on 9 September, 1944, at the Fulton Theatre in New York. This was in Lillian Hellman's great play THE SEARCHING WIND. In this very moving play of the search for truth and understanding in a troubled world, he was the conservative, once again. As always he gave a masterful performance.

His leading ladies were Cornelia Otis Skinner and Barbara O'Neill. Unfortunately for us, Mr. Diggs died less than three years later on 24 October, 1947. He was a very great loss to our theatre.

JACK DONAHUE

Of all the male dancers whom I have seen who are not ballet dancers, Mr. Donahue has always been my favorite. His Irish charm and his nimble legs were in complete rhythm and the combination was as fine as I have ever seen. Quite simply, he was born to dance.

I saw him for the first time on 24 April, 1925, at the Harris Theatre in Chicago. The play was BE YOURSELF. In this he was co-starred with Queenie Smith. It was an amusing musical but not in any sense a great one. Their numbers together were pleasing to watch and I remember one number called "The decent thing to do" which was great fun.

The next two times that I saw him he was co-starred with Marilyn Miller, and the dances between these two has never been equalled in my theatre-going. First was in SUNNY on 15 April, 1927, at the Illinois Theatre in Chicago. This beautiful show, with its lilting music and its pure joy of living, was a complete delight. Second was ROSALIE. This was at the Grand Opera House in Cincinnati on 14 January, 1929. Here the timing was perfect, but it was not quite the show that SUNNY had been. It did have some great moments, however.

The last time that I saw Jack Donahue was on 21 September, 1930, at the Shubert Theatre in Cincinnati. The show was SONS O' GUNS, in which he was starred, and he was appearing with Gina Malo as his leading lady. This was an amusing musical, and I went once again to see him and to enjoy his agility. However, he was very ill, and this became more and more obvious as the evening progressed. He managed to get through the opening night, but those of us in the audience who were his greatest admirers, knew that something was wrong. It was his last performance anywhere, as he died two days later in New York on 23 September. A great loss.

JEANNE EAGLES

Jeanne Eagles was a great actress. That she wanted to become a legend in her own time and therefore dissipated her talents and her health, was her own choice, and, unfortunately, she succeeded. Somehow, to those of us who saw her at her best, this seems to have been a great waste.

I saw her for the first time on a very hot August night, 22 August, 1923, at the Maxine Elliott Theatre in New York. (This was before the days of air-conditioning.) The play was, of course, RAIN. Her performance of Sadie Thompson was her greatest achievement. Long years of uphill struggle had made this triumph even more exhilirating. It was an electric performance in which the sparks almost ignited the audience. The stark boldness of the second act curtain shocked a great many people, because they were not prepared for the words that she used. However, in the realism of the character which she was portraying, there were no other words which would have been quite as effective. I recall also the underlying tragedy of her acceptance in having to leave under police escort to go to Australia. The constant rain on stage was a blessing in disguise to those of us in the audience, and the incessant playing of the gramophone was also very effective. Robert Kelly was the Reverend Davidson, and Robert Elliott was the Sergeant O'Hara.

Over two years later, after her long run in New York, I saw RAIN again, on 22 January, 1926 at the Harris Theatre in Chicago. She was weary, and the strain of playing the role for so many hundreds of performances was beginning to tell. However, she was an actress, and there was no let down in the exciting performance of Sadie Thompson that she was still giving. It was a great achievement.

She could have become, with discipline and constant study and growth of her innate ability, one of the greatest actresses in our American theatre. However, she chose the easy way and she died on 3 October, 1929.

EDITH EVANS

I suppose that Edith Evans has the distinction of being one of the two or three finest actresses in the English-speaking theatre. She has appeared very rarely in the United States, and then only in New York. There have been three times that I am aware of: one in 1933, EVENSONG, which had a brief run; in one of the various productions that Katharine Cornell made of ROMEO AND JULIET, she appeared as the Nurse; and the last time was in 1950, when she appeared in DAPHNE LAUREOLA which had a short life, also. This has been a great loss to our theatre.

I saw Miss Evans only once and that was in July of 1934 at the New Theatre in London. The play was THE SEA GULL of Chekov. Her performance of Irina Arkidina was the finest that I have ever seen in this role. It was masterful, full of bright wit, perfect timing, and a studied quality of vagueness which is peculiarly hers. She was surrounded by an all-star cast including Peggy Ashcroft, Stephen Haggard, Leon Quartermaine, and Alec Guiness in a small role.

I have seen her in many films and she has always given the same very articulate performance.

ELSIE FERGUSON

We come now to another actress whom I saw in a long series of silent movies in the late 1919 and 1920 periods. As an ardent movie fan, I adored Miss Elsie Ferguson. One can easily see how excited I was when she returned to the stage and I was going to be able to see her "in person". This event took place on 19 January, 1923, at the Blackstone Theatre in Chicago. The play was THE WHEEL OF LIFE. The play was something about the long boredom and the inactivity of those who have to live in places far away from their homes. The locale was India. It had a unique and mysterious quality. I have long considered that Elsie Ferguson, Ethel Barrymore, and Marjorie Rambeau were the three most beautiful women I ever saw on our stage. Miss Ferguson was as beautiful as I had remembered her, and I was not disappointed. Frederick Worlock was her leading man.

I saw her next, again at the Blackstone Theatre in Chicago, on 30 April, 1926. The play was CLOSE QUARTERS, a revival of an old play which was very amusing and quite charming. She had an all-star cast with her which included Bruce MacRae, Margaret Lawrence, and Effie Shannon. Again she stood out.

Nearly twenty years went by before I saw her again. This time was to be the last. It was on 15 October, 1943, at Fords' Theatre in Baltimore. The play was OUTRAGEOUS FORTUNE. The cast included Margalo Gillmore and Marie Ouspenskaya. They, too were excellent. Elsie Ferguson had come out of retirement to do one more play. Her response from a wide public who remembered her must have been a very pleasing and rewarding experience. She was very much the actress of the "old school" and she made the character alive and moving. One noticed the wide gestures and the quiet under-playing which were popular in her day. It was a quite successful farewell to the stage, and those of us who had seen her in years gone by were most grateful for her return.

The story that I have heard about the day after her opening night in New York has always amused me. Because of the large and talented cast they had put up no stars names on the marguee on opening night. The next morning in big lights they put up ELSIE FERGUSON! Certainly this must have been a thrill to her after so many years in returement.

MRS. FISKE

My rememberances of this very great actress begin with a childhood story. One evening in the spring of 1917, I was going downtown to see a movie. I haven't the slightest recollection of the movie I wanted to see. As I boarded the street car, about a block from my home, I met on the rear platform an older boy in his late teens, the son of family friends. We passed the time of day, and he told me that he was going down to the Majestic Theatre to see ERSTWHILE SUSAN. He planned to sit in the gallery, on the hard benches which I later came to know so well, where the price was fifty cents. Since this was only a small amount more than movies cost in those days, I asked if I could go with him. He didn't seem to mind a thirteen-year-old boy tagging along, and that is how I first became aware of the fabulous Mrs. Fiske. The date was April, 1917.

I do not recall a great deal of the performance, but I do remember that I was enchanted by the "Elocutionist from Iowa" who upset the entire household of the strict Mennonites. I was also enchanted with Mrs. Fiske. This enchantment lasted nearly fifteen years.

I next saw her at the Powers Theatre in Chicago on 22 December, 1923. The play was MARY, MARY, QUITE CONTRARY. This was a delightful comedy of manners which sparkled with wit. Mrs. Fiske as Mary Westlake (a London actress) was at her topnotch best. Her supporting company were equally fine. C. Aubrey Smith was her leading man. Francis Lister (in one of his rare American appearances) as her son Geoffrey was especially good, too. It was a great evening.

Some two years later, I saw her again, on 6 February, 1925, at the Illinois Theatre in Chicago, in a revival of THE RIVALS. Her characterization of Mrs. Malaprop was one of her greatest creations.

Six years later, I saw her for the last two times. This was in the spring of 1931. She was on tour and I saw her at the Grand Opera House in Cincinnati. She was about sixty-five years old now, and her health was failing, but her spirit and her miraculous sense of theatre never dimmed. The opening night on 6 April of LADIES OF THE JURY will long remain in my memory. Her entrance into the Jury Room as Mrs. Livingston Baldwin-Crane brought such an ovation from the sold-out house that it still rings in my ears thirty-five years later. As shrewd and accomplished an actress as she was, she was unable to speak a line for five minutes. When the applause finally subsided she made out of this foolish character a creation of wise humility, and she gave to a rather obvious and melodramatic play all her art which has never been equalled.

On 9 April, 1931 of that same week, she changed her bill to one of her many revivals of BECKY SHARP. This was her farewell to one of her greatest roles. She still played Becky with scintillating wit and wisdom. It was a masterpiece of acting. Again, my memory tells me, that when she took her curtain call her curtsey to the floor was as light as a bubble, and the entire audience stood to show their love and admiration for this great lady.

I am happy that I did not see her in her final performances in Chicago in AGAINST THE WIND, when she was much too ill to go on. I always want to remember her at her best. After a career of nearly fifty years in the American theatre she died quietly on 15 February, 1932.

PAULINE FREDERICK

Since I had seen Pauline Frederick many times in the silent films, I was much interested when she decided to return to the stage.

This thrill I experienced first on 30 September, 1922, at the Woods Theatre in Chicago. The play was THE GUILTY ONE. This was a very bad melodrama in which Miss Frederick appeared in the usual sultry role that she had made so famous in the movies. Memory does not tell me much of this performance.

I saw her next at the Cort Theatre in Chicago on 12 October, 1928. This time the play was THE IMPERFECT LADY. This was much the same type play as the one I had seen six years earlier--she was still trying to recapture her fame of the films with a role in which she could be the misunderstood woman in a minor triangle. It in no way added to her stature as an actress. It was very contrived and had little plot, and while she did the best she could, it remained rather ineffective.

The next time that I saw Pauline Frederick was again at the Cort Theatre in Chicago. The date was 26 June, 1933. The play was HER MAJESTY THE WIDOW. This was listed as a modern comedy in three acts. It was just about this and no more. Here she was trying to be a comedienne, and as in the previous plays she was out of her scope.

Fortunately, the two final times that I saw Miss Frederick she had come into her own, as she must have been in the early days of the century, when she was a favorite actress. The first of these occurred on 24 March, 1937, at the Shubert Theatre in New York. The play was THE MASQUE OF KINGS by Maxwell Anderson. She was the Empress of Austria. She was regal, and she gave a commanding and touching performance. The last time that I saw her was with Helen Hayes in MARY OF SCOTLAND, also by Maxwell Anderson.

This was on tour at the Cox Theatre in Cincinnati. Here she was the young, crafty Elizabeth I of England. This was a very fine performance; in fact, it was a better one than I had seen in New York when I first saw the play and this role had been played by Helen Menken. Miss Frederick had more of the dignity that the role required.

Miss Frederick died in 1967.

GRACE GEORGE

Grace George was one of the most charming and gracious actresses we have ever had on the American stage. Her sense of comedy was unique and her unfailing enjoyment of every role in which she appeared made her a joy to watch. She always seemed very fragile and willowy, as if a good gust of wind might blow her away.

I saw her first on 15 May, 1925, at the Studebaker Theatre in Chicago. The play was SHE HAD TO KNOW. Her leading man was Bruce MacRae. It was a frivolous comedy of a wife who wanted to learn the answer to the age old question--"Do I have attraction for another man, now that my husband has seemingly lost interest?" She found out that she had but after the thrill of the discovery she remained with her husband, who also learned to appreciate what he had nearly lost. It was an amusing play, and she was at her best.

I next saw Miss George, again in Chicago, at the Adelphi Theatre, on 21 October, 1927. Here she was in THE ROAD TO ROME, Robert Sherwood's early comedy. While I am sure that she was not as sexually seductive as Jane Cowl must have been in the role of Amytis in New York, she was her equal in all other ways. Her Hannibal was McKay Morris and together they gave outstanding performances in this truly very funny play. It was an early landmark of real comedy.

The next time that I saw Grace George was on 9 March, 1931, at the Shubert Theatre in Cincinnati. The play was THE FIRST MRS. FRAZER. (Incidentally, this was revived about twenty years later in New York with Jane Cowl in the lead--this happened to be her last performance.) But to go back, this was doubtless the best play in Miss George's long career, and the one for which she is most remembered. Here she was at the very top of her profession. She was filled with charm and the effervescence of high comedy. It was a delightful evening in the theatre and one came away with the feeling that "All's right with the world, as long as Grace George is in it."

It was thirteen years before I saw her again, this time at the National Theatre in Washington on 18 January, 1943. The play was SPRING AGAIN in which she was co-starred with C. Aubrey Smith. I had almost forgotten how lovely she could be, and in this romp she was graciousness itself. It wasn't a great play, but she made it seem very important. Her technique of comedy was at its best, and the entire evening was one of joy and pleasure.

Eight more years went by before I saw her for the last time. This was on 17 November, 1952, at the Hartman Theatre in Columbus. The play was Katharine Cornell's revival of Maugham's THE CONSTANT WIFE. I had seen it many years before with Ethel Barrymore. The director and Miss Cornell had changed the focus of the play so that Mrs. Culver (Grace George) was a major character. The curtain opened with Miss George alone on the stage and the tumultuous applause shook the rafters of the Hartman. It was a great farewell. She was past seventy years old but no one in the audience was aware of her age. She seemed ageless, and she played with as much spirit and subtle humor as ever. She died quietly a few years later and in my memory there are very few actresses who could equal her.

WILLIAM GILLETTE

I saw William Gillette only once and this was on his farewell tour of SHERLOCK HOLMES, the play that he had made famous all over the United States. The place was the Grand Opera House in Cincinnati, the date, 3 May, 1930, thirty-seven years ago.

I think that I was most impressed by his stature and his seemingly "not acting at all". I recall Booth Tarkington's praise that "he would rather see William Gillette play SHERLOCK HOLMES than be a child again on Christmas morning." He was suave, and he was a master of the art of "timing a line", always in his slow drawling voice. He moved with effortless ease, and he gave to this famous characterization his best, as always. He seemed ageless. It was a very rare treat for me to be able to have seen him, even if it was only this one time.

THE SISTERS GISH

I am writing about the Gish sisters in the same essay, because they have always seemed to be together; and, also, because I saw Dorothy only once on the stage; and I have seen Lillian many times.

DOROTHY GISH

My first impressions of Miss Gish were, naturally, many years ago, in the silent films with her sister, Lillian. Then, after quite a period of inactivity, she returned to the stage. In these first years, I was unable to see her, much to my regret. The only time that I ever saw Dorothy Gish was in the spring of 1933, at the Morosco Theatre in New York. The play was AUTUMN CROCUS in which she was starred with Francis Lederer in his first American appearance. The play, written by Dodie Smith, had a great deal of charm, and was unique in other ways, too. For example, the characters had no specific names; and Miss Gish, as "The Lady with the Spectacles", was at her very best in this role of naive vagueness, which had many overtones of those qualities one remembered from the films. There was also in her performance, a lightness of touch, and a sense of humor which made the role believable. I have always been sorry that I never had the chance to see her again. Now, in the sixties, I understand that she is not well, and it is very doubtful that she will ever be able to return.

Miss Dorothy Gish died in Italy in 1968.

LILLIAN GISH

It is especially interesting to note here that the first time that I saw "Miss Lillian" was on 14 November, 1932, also at the Morosco

Theatre in New York. The play was a revival of CAMILLE, with which she had just opened the Central City Opera House in Central City, Colorado the preceding summer. I must admit that I went with mixed emotions, as I had adored her for so many years in the silent films. I still had very fond memories of BROKEN BLOSSOMS and WAY DOWN EAST. Another reason was that, aside from the excerpt of the final act that I had seen Sarah Bernhardt do on her farewell tour some fifteen years before, I had never seen CAMILLE on the stage. When I left the theatre my emotions were still mixed. She did not, at that time, possess a truly fine and melodious voice, and there was a listlessness about her acting. However, she was pictorially beautiful; and there were times, in the garden scene at Auteuil and in the final scene, in which she had gleaming moments, and her frail innocence seemed to light up the entire stage. Raymond Hackett was a handsome and convincing Armand Duval, and Cora Witherspoon was wonderful as Prudence.

The next time that I saw Lillian Gish was on 12 April, 1938, at the Grand Opera House in Chicago. The play was Maxwell Anderson's THE STAR-WAGON, in which she was starred with Burgess Meredith. Much had happened since the time that I had seen her six years before. She had grown in depth of character, she had been under the best teachers in New York to acquire the lovely speaking voice which she now possessed, and, all in all, she was now the actress that everyone knew she could be. In this strange play of the "time machine", she was required to play a middle-aged housewife, and then to go backwards into the early part of the century. At this time she was a young girl in the small church choir, and in the scene following, she attended the Sunday School picnic. In

In each period of the play she was at her best. It was a warm and human performance. Mr. Meredith was at his charming best, too, and it was a very rewarding evening in the theatre.

The next time that I saw her was in the spring of 1940. This was at the Blackstone Theatre in Chicago. She was now playing Vinnie in LIFE WITH FATHER, with Percy Waram. This is the finest performance that I have ever seen her give. Of all the actresses who have played Vinnie, and I have seen several, Lillian Gish's was by far the best. Every moment she was on the stage she was a joy to watch and to hear. She was lovable, and she was innocence touched with wisdom.

Two years later, on 26 October, 1942, I saw her at the National Theatre in Washington, D. C. This time the play was a pre-Broadway tour of MR. SYCAMORE. This strange play, about a man who desired to be a tree, was short-lived. It really never arrived anywhere, and it was very confusing. Miss Gish, as the wife, was as confused as the play. I fear that it added little to her credits as an actress. Stuart Erwin, of the films, was "the man". Interesting, too, was the return to the stage, after many years, of Claiborne Foster, although she did not last through the tryout period.

It was nine years before I saw Miss Gish again. This was on 26 August, 1951. She was now in summer stock at the Salt Creek Theatre in Hinsdale, Illinois. She was getting ready for Broadway a play called MISS MABLE. It, unfortunately, never reached New York. It was an amusing play, but left very little that I can recall. Miss Gish was convincing, charming, and winning, but even she could not save a rather weak play.

Another nine years went by before I saw Miss Gish again. This was in June, 1970, at the Belasco Theatre in New York, in ALL THE WAY HOME, a very beautiful and heartwarming play dramatized from James Agee's novel, A DEATH IN THE FAMILY. Miss Gish played the aunt, the one who was partially deaf, and she gave to the role all of her finest qualities. While it was really a small part, it seemed to stand out. The cast was brilliant in every way. The memory of the entire performance remains with me as one of the truly great evenings in the theatre.

I saw Miss Gish again in January, 1968, at the Forrest Theatre in Philadelphia. This was in Robert Anderson's beautiful play, I NEVER SANG FOR MY FATHER. Her role in the play was brief, as she died early in the play. However she was as wistful and charming as ever. Her few moments on the stage were beautifully played.

Next I saw Miss Gish on 17 October, 1971, at the Walnut Theatre in Philadelphia. This was a lecture, which she illustrated with scenes from many of her famous roles in the silent films. It was a complete joy and, as we know that she is in her early seventies, she is a marvel.

At any time that I can, I shall always go to see Lillian Gish in whatever she happens to be playing. Time has been most kind to her, and from a friend of mine who has been in her company and has rehearsed with her, I hear that she is remarkably agile and ever young.

I have been fortunate, too, to get a copy of her autobiography. It is most revealing and very interesting to read.

SYDNEY GREENSTREET

My memories of Mr. Greenstreet cover a very wide span of years--over forty--and a wide scope of characterization, from musicals to serious dramatic performances. There was something unique about his large, solid stature which gave him a commanding appearance in any role that he chose to play. His smile could be sinister; it could, also, be warm and winning.

I saw him for the first time on 28 September, 1924, at the Illinois Theatre in Chicago. The show was THE MAGIC RING, a musical with the effervescent Mitzi as its star. In this he played the role of the owner of an antique shop. I recall that he was urbane and charming. The cast also included Jeannette MacDonald, who rose to such great heights in the films a few years later.

The next two times that I saw Sydney Greenstreet occurred during a split week of 3 February, 1929, at the Grand Opera House in Cincinnati. He appeared first as Kublai, the Great Khan, in Eugene O'Neill's MARCO MILLIONS. Earle Larrimore was the Marco. This is not one of Mr. O'Neill's outstanding plays, but it had its colorful and exciting moments. Later that same week, he appeared in the title role of Ben Jonson's VOLPONE. Here he was at his best, and he gave a very subtle and delightful performance. This is a great romp, and he was having a wonderful time.

I next saw him, again at the Grand Opera House in Cincinnati, on 26 October, 1931. This time he was playing Lord Loam in a revival of Sir James Barrie's THE ADMIRABLE CHRICHTON. He gave his special gifts of pure comedy to this foolish part and he made him seem a pompous, well-meaning "busy body", rather than a caricature, as the role is sometimes played. The stars were Walter Hampden and Fay Bainter.

When I saw him next he was back in musical comedy. This was at the Shubert Theatre in Cincinnati. The date was 3 December, 1934. The show was ROBERTA, one of the really memorable musicals. It starred Tamara, and featured Fay Templeton in her farewell to the stage. Mr. Greenstreet played Lord Henry Delves, listed as a friend of Roberta. Here he was in a smaller role but he made it stand out. The hit number of the show was, of course, "Smoke Gets in Your Eyes", sung by Tamara, and it is still very popular thirty-odd years later.

Sydney Greenstreet was in the company of The Lunts the next five times that I saw him. This was over a period of several years, and in widely different places.

On 29 April, 1935, he appeared as Baptista in Shakespeare's THE TAMING OF THE SHREW, at the Cox Theatre in Cincinnati. The role is not as foolish as the role of Lord Loam in CHRICHTON, and he gave it the dignity that a Shakespearean role requires. The Lunts were hilarious, and the entire performance was done in a modern vein and was very funny.

On 29 June, 1936, I saw him at the Shubert Theatre in New York. This time he was in Robert Sherwood's IDIOT'S DELIGHT. He was playing Dr. Waldersee. Here, again, he was in a more serious and a much more sinister role. He was excellent.

I saw him next during Christmas week at the Erlanger Theatre in Chicago. This time he was in AMPHITRYON '38, in which he played The Trumpeter. Here he was back again in one of his very subtle and amusing characterizations.

Next we go back to Cincinnati again, where I saw him on 14 April, 1939, at the Taft Theatre. Now he was playing Peter Sorin, in Chekov's

THE SEA GULL, again the more subdued and studied character. Aside from the Lunts, this cast brought to the theatre the young Uta Hagen as Nina.

The last time that I saw Mr. Greenstreet was on 27 December, 1940, at the Grand Opera House in Chicago. The play was Robert Sherwood's THERE SHALL BE NO NIGHT. Here the worldly wisdom and humility that he gave to the character of Uncle Waldemar was truly a fitting climax to the long list of roles that I had seen him play. To me this was his finest performance.

Of his long list of films, I recall best his performances in CASABLANCA and the MALTESE FALCON.

He was a great actor and he gave something to the American stage which is very difficult to recapture, his vitality, his talent, and his undeniable charm.

MITZI HAJOS

Of all of the soubrettes who have come out of Vienna, or was it Budapest, to the United States, Mitzi Hajos was by far the most famous. Not long after she had achieved fame in our country she dropped the Hajos and became simply Mitzi throughout her long and varied career. I have always thought it was because very few could pronounce her last name.

I saw her for the first time in May of 1918 at the Metropolitan Theatre in Minneapolis. The play was POM POM. She had been playing in this show for some time, and now she was on tour. It was a comic opera of the old school, with a circus background. My memories do not recall very much of the performance.

I saw her next on 16 January, 1921, at the Majestic Theatre in Peoria. The play was LADY BILLY. Here, she was playing an impoverished Countess who, dressed in boy's clothes, exhibited her castle to foreign visitors (mostly American); she fell in love with an American engineer who caused her to abandon her disguise and become the "girl" that she really was. Her leading man--and later her husband--was Boyd Marshall. He appeared with her in all of her subsequent performances.

The next time that I saw her was on 28 September, 1924, at the Illinois Theatre in Chicago. The play, THE MAGIC RING. There was never a great deal of variety in a Mitzi show; they followed the same pattern, but they were always entertaining and enjoyable. This time she was surrounded by a terrific cast including Sydney Greenstreet, Boyd Marshall, and Jeanette MacDonald.

I saw her again about a year later on 11 October, 1925, at the Apollo

Theatre in Chicago. This was in NAUGHTY RIQUETTE. This time she was a French "singer of songs" with a past that was somewhat questionable but pure in the sense of musical comedy. Stanley Lupino was her leading man, and it was one of the few times that she appeared without her husband, Boyd Marshall.

Five years went by before I saw her for the last time. This was on 30 March, 1930, at the Grand Opera House in Cincinnati. This was toward the end of her career and she chose as her farewell, SARI, which had been one of her most famous roles--one that she had played in all of the capitals of Europe as well as in the United States. It was a charming production, filled with all of the old time pleasures of the early type of musical show. "The Sari Waltz" is a haunting tune and she was still able to sing it with verve and a lovely feeling of romance and love. Boyd Marshall was again her leading man and the comedy role was wonderfully played by Arthur Treacher. He was great as always.

Mitzi was never a great star of the stage, but she was always a pleasant and enjoyable one. She gave humor and a pleasing sense of relaxation to her many hundreds of admirers.

WALTER HAMPDEN

Walter Hampden has had a long and distinguished career in the American theatre. He was a classic actor of the old school. He had a commanding stature, a big powerful voice, and a sure knowledge of theatre.

I saw Mr. Hampden for the first time on 16 June, 1924, at the National Theatre in New York. He was playing the title role in Rostand's CYRANO de BERGERAC. It was the first time that I had seen this famous romantic tragedy and I was completely thrilled with the production. I had just graduated from high school and I was on a trip to New York as a graduation present. This was a great experience for me, as I had long looked forward to seeing this performance. I was not disappointed. It was a great theatrical experience. In this production the young and charming Caroll McComas was the Roxane.

It was seven years before I saw him again. This time was on 26 October, 1931, at the Grand Theatre in Cincinnati. He was now playing the part of Crichton in the revival of Barrie's THE ADMIRABLE CRICHTON. He gave the part a perfect dignity and he made the "perfect butler" a real human being. Fay Bainter was the charming Lady Mary.

For the next several years he toured the country in a series of great roles. He came each year to Cincinnati, so that the performances that follow are all in the same place but in different years.

On 4 November, 1932, I saw him once again as Cyrano in CYRANO de BERGERAC. This was at the Shubert Theatre. His wit and his complete mastery of the role had not dimmed. It was a commanding performance. This time it was the lovely Katherine Warren who played the Roxane.

Next, on 27 February, 1933, he played a split week at the Shubert Theatre in Cincinnati. First he appeared in CAPONSACCHI, a play made from Browning's THE RING AND THE BOOK. This was one of his best performances and he was excellent. Later the same week, on 1 March, 1933, I was finally able to see him as Hamlet in Shakespeare's HAMLET. Mr. Hampden's was a studied and morose characterization, notable for the melody in his voice, and in the reading of the Shakespearean verse. He had none of the virility and the excitement of the modern conceptions of Hamlet. But it was an interesting characterization, nevertheless. This was an especially interesting performance because Evelyn Venable was just getting started in the theatre, and her experience with Mr. Hampden was the crowning moment of her early career. She appeared as Ophelia. She had only recently graduated from Walnut Hills High School in Cincinnati, where I was now teaching English and Drama. We were all naturally thrilled with Miss Venable's achievement. She was very fine in the role, young as she was at the time.

I saw Mr. Hampden next on 3 January, 1934, at the Cox Theatre in Cincinnati. The play was a revival of this great classic, and in a new translation. He was powerful, as always, and he gave the role great dignity and finesse.

It was seven years before I saw him again. This time it was on 27 November, 1941, at the Taft Theatre in Cincinnati. This time he was taking a "busman's holiday" and he was appearing as Sir Anthony Absolute in a revival of THE RIVALS. It was an all-star revival with Mary Boland as Mrs. Malaprop, and Bobby Clark as Bob Acres. It was a riot, and everyone was having such a good time in this old play.

The last time that I saw Mr. Hampden was on 21 February, 1944 at the Studebaker Theatre in Chicago. I was on leave from the Navy and I was in Chicago at this time. The play was THE PATRIOTS, Sidney Kingsley's play about Thomas Jefferson. He was very compelling in the role and it was a good climax to a long and remarkable career in the theatre. This time the role of the daughter was played by Julie Haydon. I had seen the play previously in New York, with an unknown actor in the role of Jefferson, and the role of the daughter had been played by Madge Evans. His contributions to the American theatre were monumental. He was a great force in our theatre for many years.

ANN HARDING

As I write of my memories of Miss Harding, I realize that the only two times that I saw her were both over forty years ago.

I saw Ann Harding for the first time on 26 April, 1925, at the Selwyn Theatre in Chicago. The play was THE GREEN HAT starring Katharine Cornell and Leslie Howard. As Venice, the second leading lady, she was delightful, and also very beautiful. She had not achieved the status that she acquired a few years later, but she was definitely an actress to watch. This was a pre-Broadway production and when it did arrive in New York her role was taken over by Margalo Gillmore. No real explanation has ever been given for the change.

By the second time that I saw her, on 30 August, 1928 at the Adelphi Theatre, again in Chicago, she had arrived and was a most accomplished actress. The play was one that made her famous, THE TRIAL OF MARY DUGAN. In this court room melodrama her blonde beauty, and her complete mastery of her role in this somewhat contrived play, carried her into a new and long career. Miss Harding was a sensitive and sincere actress. She was never "showy" and her fame here and in a long series of films made her very much admired.

She has returned, in the last few years, both on the stage and in the films, but I have not been able to see her. I remember her as a beautiful woman who was never really appreciated in our theatre.

SIR CEDRIC HARDWICKE

The death of Sir Cedric Hardwicke a few years ago closed the career of a very fine character actor. He had a quality of acting which was entirely his own. There was always a certain coldness--to some extent an aloofness--about him that set him apart from all other actors.

I saw him first during the season of 1939 when he was on tour in SHADOW AND SUBSTANCE. This was at the Cox Theatre in Cincinnati. The cast included the very great actress, Sara Allgood, and Julie Haydon. As the aging priest he had a mellowness, and a wise and carefully thought out characterization. It was a very beautiful play, and I remember it with pleasure.

I saw him next, again at the Cox Theatre in Cincinnati. The date was 21 January, 1946. This time he was in the pre-Broadway tour of ANTIGONE AND THE TYRANT, in which he was co-starred with Katharine Cornell. This new version of the ancient Greek tragedy, done in modern dress on an almost empty stage, was most interesting to see. Sir Cedric's Creon was a beautifully planned characterization, and he gave it great dignity.

The last time that I planned to see Sir Cedric Hardwicke was supposed to be with Gertrude Berg in A MAJORITY OF ONE at the Shubert Theatre in Cincinnati, at a Saturday matinee on 17 February, 1961. However, I was ill at the time, and my wife attended with a friend so that I might learn, through her good eyes and ears, all about this performance. She has been my "second on the aisle" for many years, and her report was all to the good. He was as suave and charming as ever. We shall miss him very much.

ANNA HELD

That Anna Held made a place for herself in the American theatre in the early part of the twentieth century is a foregone conclusion. She was exotic, she was French, and she had the most beautiful eyes, which she used to great advantage. She was always "news" in those early days, and everything she did on or off stage seemed to be good copy. In spite of, or because of, all this publicity, she was a really fine musical comedy comedienne.

I saw her only once and that was during the season of 1916-17, at the Majestic Theatre in Peoria. The musical was called FOLLOW ME. In this she had her usual role of a soubrette which was common in those days. The musical was unimportant; however, after all of these years there is one moment that I do remember when she dropped the role she was playing and became herself. Here she was the perfect musical hall singer, and I was thrilled with her old favorites: "WON'T YOU COME AND PLAY WIZ ME?" and "I CAN'T MAKE MY EYES BEHAVE". In her cast, my program tells me, was the young Edith Day who became one of our most accomplished musical comedy stars. In later years, she became a very fine actress.

Since I was but thirteen years old when I saw her, the memory is dim; but even now I can remember these songs, and the piquant manner in which she sang them. She was a legend in her own time, and she died, quite young, during the following summer, 1918, in New York.

RAYMOND HITCHCOCK

Raymond Hitchcock was a comedian of the old school. He had a rasping voice and his comedy technique came from his personal appearance. He seemed always to look like something of a bum, with one shock of blonde hair over his eye.

I saw him first during the season 1918-19 in a revue called HITCHY KOO at the Majestic Theatre in Peoria. Here he was the song and dance man surrounded by pretty girls. He was funny, but never the equal of many other comedians such as Leon Errol or Charles Butterworth; nor did he ever have the timeless quality that made W. C. Fields so great. I recall very little of this performance. However, I do remember a young girl named Lee Morse who sang sultry songs; I have never heard of her since, but she was an excellent example of the early blues singer.

The only other time that I saw Mr. Hitchcock was in the spring of 1924, again at the Majestic Theatre in Peoria. He was now in a straight comedy role, in the road company of the play THE OLD SOAK. Here he played Clem Hawley, an amiable old codger who was addicted to the bottle but who possessed a lovable philosophical character, nevertheless. It was played with amusing overtones, and it was most enjoyable. I found him to be much better in a straight part.

Mr. Hitchcock died in 1929 in California.

WILLIAM HODGE

There was a special quality about Mr. Hodge which endeared him to a large and faithful following. Perhaps his following came from the type of plays which he wrote and in which he appeared. These were all family plays, in which good always triumphed, and there seemed to be no evil in the world. Righteousness and good will were in abundance. There were never any moments that could be considered even remotely suggestive. Sex was a subject that he never touched upon. In many ways he was the heart and soul of the midwestern American idea of his generation.

I saw him first on 1 March, 1921, at the Majestic Theatre in Peoria. The play was THE GUEST OF HONOR. I was entertained by the homespun humor in the play, and the fact that William Hodge seemed to be a great favorite. Ann Davis was in his supporting cast.

The only other time that I saw Mr. Hodge was on 21 January, 1923, at the Studebaker Theatre in Chicago. The play was FOR ALL OF US. The theme was much the same as that of the former play--only the characters and the situations in which they found themselves had changed. Of course, everything came out all right in the end.

In spite of all of the above, I still feel that he had a very definite place in the American theatre, and he appealed to a very wide and very enthusiastic audience.

MIRIAM HOPKINS

Miss Hopkins is something of an enigma in our theatre. No one can doubt her physical appeal. There is a sultry "southern belle" quality about her that is evident in every role in which she appears. She enters the stage in a whirlwind, and her bright and witty banter never seems to diminish. She is certainly not a great actress, but she is assuredly a mighty exciting one. I am sure that I will never miss a chance to see her whenever she happens to be around. Unfortunately, this chance is becoming less and less frequent these days.

I saw Miriam Hopkins for the first time on 2 January, 1938, at the Erlanger Theatre in Chicago. The play was WINE OF CHOICE. As the title suggests, the choice was between three men--Leslie Banks, Donald Cook, and Theodore Newton, none of whom were entirely satisfactory, so that in the end she returns to her search for happiness. Miss Hopkins was aided in this mediocre nonsense by Alexander Woollcott, who was making his first stage appearance. Even he couldn't save the play, but Miss Miriam was a delight to look at, and to listen to, also.

I saw her next on 10 February, 1944, at the Locust Theatre in Philadelphia. The play was THE PERFECT MARRIAGE. I fear this was an even more disastrous failure. It never even attempted Broadway. However, again Miss Hopkins was most engaging.

I next saw her on 26 December, 1945, at the Studebaker Theatre in Chicago. The play was ST. LAZAR'S PHARMACY. This one didn't make it, either. However, it did have a somewhat better plot than MARRIAGE, and it was imaginatively and beautifully staged. Miss Hopkins, too, was at her very best, and she gave a winning and sensitive performance.

The last time that I saw Miriam Hopkins was on 18 August, 1951, at the Salt Creek Theatre in Hinsdale, Illinois. The play, an even worse trifle, was called TOLD TO THE CHILDREN. It had something to do with "free love" and its subsequent issues, all involved somewhere along the line with birth control. It never made Broadway, either. I was primarily interested in an old student of mine, John Newland, who was in the cast, and because of his many T. V. productions he had second billing over the established actor, Bramwell Fletcher, who was also involved. My old student, Jack, was adequate, charming, and handsome, but little else. Miss Hopkins tried hard, and she was lovely, but all to no avail. Young Newland was kind enough to introduce us to Miss Hopkins, when we went back stage to see him. She was even more electric and enchanting than I had imagined. She was gracious and most unaffected. To paraphrase Mr. Woollcott--regardless of these failures, I will travel several miles, if necessary, to see her whenever she appears.

LESLIE HOWARD

Leslie Howard had so many qualities that endeared him to the American public, that even though he never lost his British touch he seemed to be a very vital part of the American theatre. His long residence in the United States, either in the theatre in New York or in the films in Hollywood, made for him a wide and adoring public. He had a masterful ability to underplay a role, which made him seem, at times, not to be acting at all. In a sense he was a matinee idol, but it was an appelation which he fortunately overcame.

I saw him for the first time when I was quite young, on 20 August, 1923, at the Gaiety Theatre in New York. The play was AREN'T WE ALL starring Cyril Maude. Mr. Howard was appearing for the first time in America in a somewhat stylized role of the other man in a typical triangle. It was, of course, a play written for the many talents and personal charm of Mr. Maude, and he was at his best. Leslie Howard was somewhat overpowered in the small role that he played, but he nevertheless stood out.

I saw him next the following spring, 1924, at the Blackstone Theatre in Chicago. Here he was playing the disguised prince in JUST SUPPOSE, with Patricia Collinge and Geoffrey Kerr. This was an amusing play written about a supposed visit of the Prince of Wales to a Virginia plantation in the United States. He was definitely coming into his own, and he gave a charming performance. He had most assuredly arrived, and he was a very busy leading man by now.

I next saw Mr. Howard on 26 April, 1925, at the Selwyn Theatre in Chicago. The play was the pre-Broadway performance of THE GREEN HAT. In this he was appearing with Katharine Cornell and Ann Harding. This was his most serious role to date, and he played it with a feeling of sureness and a wonderful sense of timing. He, also, had sincere pathos, when the role demanded it. It was a beautiful performance and one that I shall long remember.

I saw him next on 20 June, 1932, at the Empire Theatre in New York. The play was THE ANIMAL KINGDOM. Now he was a full-fledged star in his own right. This was one of his finest performances, and he became the idol of many. He had a wide following. He was supported by Lora Baxter, William Harrigan, and Ilka Chase.

Perhaps the fondest memory of Leslie Howard that I have, was in the next performance in which I saw him. This was on 28 June, 1935, at the Broadhurst Theatre in New York. The play was THE PETRIFIED FOREST. His poignant understanding of the role of the "lost" man (Squire) was to me his finest performance in our theatre. Of course, the play itself was one of Robert Sherwood's best, and its overtones of purely American idiosyncrasies were amusing but also pathetic. His supporting cast included Humphrey Bogart, Peggy Conklin, and an old silent movie star, Blanche Sweet. (It was good to see her again, after many years.)

I saw Leslie Howard for the last time on 27 December, 1936, at the Grand Opera House in Chicago. He was playing HAMLET with Mary Servoss as Gertrude and Pamela Stanley as Ophelia. I do not agree with John Mason Brown and some of our other critics that this was one of our worst performances of Hamlet. I think that it was much more exciting than many other Hamlets that I have seen. True it was not Mr. Howard's best role, nor did he give it the great deal of variety that the part demands; however, he did read many of the speeches well, and he was handsome, lithe, and agile, but he never reached any specific heights of greatness. I have always thought that the real problem of this performance, was it was done at the wrong time. John Gielgud had just opened in New York with his masterful and well-acclaimed production of HAMLET which set the critics and the public on edge. Mr. Howard followed this performance by a few weeks, and there was no comparison. If he had done HAMLET at any other time, I am sure that it would have received a far more favorable reception.

He made many films in Hollywood and I recall best the following: THE SCARLET PIMPERNELL, his Ashley in GONE WITH THE WIND, THE ANIMAL KINGDOM, and THE PETRIFIED FOREST. In all of these he was at his very finest.

His untimely death when his plane was shot down by enemy aircraft occurred on 1 June, 1943. He will long be remembered by all who saw him.

HENRY HULL

Henry Hull, coming from the famous Hull family of Louisville, Kentucky, was the most widely acclaimed of the three brothers. The eldest, Warren, never achieved great fame--he became the husband of Margaret Anglin; Shelly had a brief and very promising career, and was becoming a very fine young actor when he died at an early age. His widow, Josephine Hull, became one of the greatest of all of our American comediennes. Mr. Hull was for a long time a perennial juvenile. He had good looks, great charm, and he was a very popular leading man. Fortunately, for me, I did not see Henry Hull until quite some time after this first early period in which he appeared in a series of inconsequential comedies.

I saw him for the first time on 29 December, 1930, at the National Theatre in New York. The play was GRAND HOTEL. This famous play gave him the chance to show the real ability that he had. He appeared with Eugenie Leontovich, and their scenes together were beautifully played.

I saw him next on 20 December, 1932, at the Blackstone Theatre in Chicago. The play was SPRINGTIME FOR HENRY. This is an amusing trifle, but a really very funny play.

I saw him next on 20 June, 1934, at the 48th Street Theatre in New York. Here he was the Jetter Lester in TOBACCO ROAD. This play, unfortunately, fell into the hands of unscrupulous managers during its long run, where it was advertised as a "sex-orgy". However, in its original production, it was a tragic comedy of the folk lore of a pathetic group of underprivileged people. Mr. Hull was superb in the original production. Gone was the veneer of the slick comedy role; here was real acting. He was supported by Margaret Wycherly, a well-known and able character actress. About two years later, on 5 January, 1936, I saw TOBACCO ROAD again, at the Cox Theatre in Cincinnati. Mr. Hull's performance had lost none of its vitality and none of its sincerity. There were many cast changes, but the touring cast was very satisfactory.

The next time that I saw Henry Hull was on 24 March, 1937, at the Shubert Theatre in New York. This was in Maxwell Anderson's THE MASQUE OF KINGS. In this drama he was playing Prince Rudolf. He was dignified and very moving in this role. It was one of the highlights of his long career. This was a fine, sensitive play of the tragedy of Mayerling, outside Vienna, during the reign of the Hapsburgs. His forceful performance matched the play. Included in the cast were Dudley Diggs, Margo, and Pauline Frederick.

The next time that I saw Henry Hull was on 17 November, 1941, at the Cox Theatre in Cincinnati. This was in a pre-Broadway performance of a play called PLAY WITH FIRE. It was a very mediocre play, and certainly it did not lend itself to the stature of Mr. Hull as an actor. As I recall, it never reached Broadway.

The last time that I saw Henry Hull was on 26 February, 1945, at the National Theatre in Washington, D. C. The play was FOOLISH NOTION. Here he was playing with Talullah Bankhead. The play was not up to the usual standard that we were led to expect from Philip Barry; but it did give Mr. Hull a good part, and he played it with relish.

In his death, a few years ago, we lost one of our most hard-working and glamorous stars. His long career on the stage was seldom, if ever, dull.

GLENN HUNTER

The tragedy of Glenn Hunter lies in the fact that he achieved great fame at an early age, appeared in at least two great performances, and then was never able to find another great role in which to make a comeback. The last years of his life were spent in much frustration and unhappiness, due to his appearance in many poor plays which had very short runs.

The first time that I saw Glenn Hunter was when he was in the cast of THE INTIMATE STRANGERS. This was at the Powers Theatre in Chicago during the season of 1922. Here he was in the small role of Johnny White, a typical young man of the period. He showed much promise. The stars were Billie Burke and Alfred Lunt.

The next time that I saw Mr. Hunter he had come into his own as an important star, to be watched with interest. This was on 24 August, 1923, at the Cort Theatre in New York. The play was MERTON OF THE MOVIES. This was a very well-written play, a satire on the movies. It had humility and a complete understanding of the "moviestruck" boy from the middle west who comes to Hollywood, as a young man with visions of becoming a great emotional star. It becomes evident that his "emoting" causes great laughter in the audience, and he is smart enough to see the chance of success in this other medium. The only other person in the cast who was sincere in her befriending of the young man was the "Montague Girl". She was played by Florence Nash. Her performance was a gem. This put Mr. Hunter on the top and it had a long run.

I saw him next during the season of 1924 at the Blackstone Theatre in Chicago. This was in a revival of SHE STOOPS TO CONQUER. Mr. Hunter played the role of Tony Lumpkin. He played the old role with understanding and charm. He gave it humor and a certain naivete which made it unique. He never overplayed this foolish character, and he was very believable. The cast included Mrs. Leslie Carter, Patricia Collinge, and Fay Bainter.

The last time that I saw Glenn Hunter was in his greatest success. This was, of course, YOUNG WOODLEY. I saw it during the season of 1926, at the Blackstone Theatre in Chicago. This moving tragi-comedy with very definite overtones was sensitively written and beautifully played. It was a great achievement for a young and promising actor. The very fine and beautiful Helen Gahagan was with him in this cast.

However, his light failed, and never again in the theatre did he reach the heights of this play. This was a tragic loss as he had so much to offer. He died on 30 December, 1945, almost twenty years after his greatest success.

WALTER HUSTON

There was an undeniable maleness, a feeling of honesty and fair play that lent a certain ruggedness to Walter Huston. He was not a great actor but he had an infectious personality which came across the footlights to make him one of the best-loved of all of our actors.

I first saw him during the season of 1935-1936 at the Shubert Theatre in New York. The play was DODSWORTH. As Sam Dodsworth, he represented all of the middle class successful American business men. He was well liked, had many friends, a successful business, and this trip to Europe was his first real vacation. It was a very real characterization. Fran Dodsworth was played by Fay Bainter in one of her best performances. About a year later, I saw DODSWORTH again, on 30 March, 1936, at the Shubert Theatre in Cincinnati. He played the role with just as much understanding and charm as before. Nan Sunderland was now the Fran Dodsworth. She did not have the brittle quality of Miss Bainter, but she was very fine in the role.

The next time that I saw Mr. Huston was on a night in April, 1939 at the Cox Theatre in Cincinnati. This was in KNICKERBOCKER HOLIDAY. The performance was a pure delight. His Peter Stuyvesant was a great characterization, and his advent into musical comedy was made with great ease. When he sang "September Song", the entire audience cheered. It was a fine, gay, and festive evening in the theatre.

It was almost ten years before I saw him again, unfortunately, for the last time. This was on 10 February, 1947, again at the Cox Theatre in Cincinnati. The play was THE APPLE OF HIS EYE. This was an amusing bit of homespun comedy. He played his role with his usual charm. But there was little to work on. He did his best with a really rather poor script. At the curtain call he signaled to the orchestra in the pit--and repeated "September Song" from his former hit show. This, alone, was worth the evening.

His death on 7 April, 1950 was a very great loss to the American theatre. His son, John Huston, carries on very ably in Hollywood as one of our better film directors.

FRIEDA INESCORT

There is a quality of dignity about Miss Inescort which never seems to leave her, no matter what role she happens to be playing. This quiet reserve is coupled with a poise and beauty which are hard to describe. I have always admired her as an actress, even though I only saw her three times over a very wide span of years.

I first saw Frieda Inescort on 15 October, 1928, at the Shubert Theatre in Cincinnati. She was the Portia with George Arliss in Shakespeare's THE MERCHANT OF VENICE. She read the lines with ease in a beautiful speaking voice. She gave the role compassion and, at times, moments of wonderful humor--especially in the "casket scene". Her dignity was most outstanding in the "quality of mercy" speech.

I saw her next during Christmas week of 1932, at the Royale Theatre in New York. The play was WHEN LADIES MEET. Here she was the "other woman" playing with Selina Royal and Spring Byington. It was one of Rachael Crothers' best comedies of manners. She was excellent in her quiet way.

Twelve years went by before I saw her again. This was on 25 September, 1944, at the National Theatre in Washington, D. C. The play was SOLDIER'S WIFE. While the stars were Martha Scott and Myron McCormick, Miss Inescort, along with Glenn Anders, managed to keep up their end of the comedy dialogue. She was a complete joy to watch and to hear.

I assume that she is now in retirement as I have not heard of her in many years. She has always held a special place for me among my favorite actresses.

ELSIE JANIS

Elsie Janis was one of our most popular and well known musical comedy stars. Her career covers a period of many years. She was starred in outstanding musicals before World War I and then during the war she became one of our most beloved entertainers to go overseas to entertain the soldiers. The fame that she created by these tours never really left her, and when she returned to the United States she was already a legend.

I saw Miss Janis only once and that was on 25 September, 1925, at the Harris Theatre in Chicago. The Revue was called PUZZLES OF 1925. She had many chances to reveal her peculiar charm and to create good humor for her audiences. Much of the time she appeared in tweeds and a top hat. She was vivacious and very winning. I had heard so much about her through the years, that I was quite captivated by her mimicry and her complete abandon. This revue had two other well known comedians in the cast, Jimmy Hussy and Helen Broderick.

AL JOLSON

I suppose one of the most famous and one of the most loved of our comedians over the years has always been Al Jolson. He possessed a magnetic quality, a great sense of humor, and a brassy singing voice-- all of these qualities gave great pleasure to many thousands of people. He was completely unique in the sense that no one else has ever been quite like him. His songs dripped sentimentality and bathos, but his public loved him.

I saw him only once on the stage, during the 1918-19 season at the Majestic Theatre in Peoria. The musical comedy was called SINBAD. In this he introduced "Mammy", one of his most famous songs; he sang it down on one knee. His traditional black face and white gloves became a legend in his own time.

I saw him, of course, in the first really important "talkie", THE JAZZ SINGER in the early thirties at the Capitol Theatre in Cincinnati. It was a joy to see him in this new medium, and he once again sang all of the songs for which he had been famous throughout his long career.

Mr. Jolson died in San Francisco in 1950.

MADGE KENNEDY

Just a little over a year ago (September 1965) I was made aware of an actress of whom I had not heard in many years. In a short-lived little play that Ruth Gordon wrote, A VERY RICH WOMAN, who should turn up in the cast but Madge Kennedy. This was along with Miss Gordon herself, who played the leading role, of course. It is interesting to note, here, that everyone in the cast was past seventy years old!

My memories of Madge Kennedy go back thirty-five years. I saw her for the first time on 1 March, 1931, at the Shubert Theatre in Cincinnati. This was in A. A. Milne's MICHAEL AND MARY. This has long been one of my favorite plays, and I was not disappointed in the production. In fact, Madge Kennedy as Mary was all I could have wished in the role. She gave it great sincerity and humility. Terrence O'Neil was the Michael, and he was equally fine. Harry Beresford, as the policeman, P. C. Tuff, was wonderful.

I saw her again the following summer on 22 June, 1931, at the Times Square Theatre in New York. The play was Noel Coward's PRIVATE LIVES. Miss Kennedy and Otto Kruger had taken over the roles made famous by Gertrude Lawrence and Noel Coward. No one expected Miss Kennedy to be Gertrude Lawrence (no one could be) but many of us were surprised and very pleased that she was as fine an Amanda as she was. She had her own caustic wit and charm, and she had a wonderful comedy sense. Her timing was perfect, and even her singing of "Some Day I'll Find You" in Act II was simply and sincerely done. It was a joyous romp and loads of fun. I saw it again when she took it on tour during the season of 1932-1933 at the Grand Theatre in Cincinnati. I enjoyed it all over again, as much as I had in New York.

The last time that I saw Miss Kennedy was on 7 January, 1934 at the Cox Theatre in Cincinnati. She was now in the road company of AUTUMN CROCUS. In this she was supported by Rollo Peters. Here, again she was following another actress in the leading role, in this case Dorothy Gish, (whom I had seen in the role in New York). Because she is a wise and intelligent actress in her own right, she never copies another's style. She gave to the "Lady With the Spectacles" her own winsome charm, and it was a beautiful performance. Mr. Peters, whom I had not seen in many years, not since his Romeo with Jane Cowl, in fact, was dashing and persuasive.

It is no wonder, then, that after a lapse of thirty years it was interesting to see that she was making a come back in the theatre. Yes, I am sorry that I didn't get to see A VERY RICH WOMAN. I would like very much to have seen Madge Kennedy once again.

FRANCINE LARRIMORE

Francine Larrimore possessed a certain quality which made her an actress who was always interesting to watch on our stage. She had a quality of abandon which was in keeping with the type of roles she played during the 1920's. She was vibrant and alive, she had an interesting throaty voice, and in those early days she had striking red hair.

I saw Miss Larrimore for the first time on 27 December, 1921, at the Cort Theatre in Chicago. The play was NICE PEOPLE by Rachael Crothers. It was a very amusing comedy of the somewhat lax morals of the day, and she gave to her role a great deal of appeal and charm. As a spoiled debutante she overstepped the code of the period, and she got by with it. Robert Ames was her leading man and he, too, was very fine.

I saw her next on 23 January, 1925, at the Princess Theatre, again in Chicago. The play was PARASITES. While it was not as good a play as the former, it did have Miss Larrimore, and with her it had sparkle and zest. Her leading man was Austin Fairman.

The last time that I saw Francine Larrimore she was giving one of the best performances of her career. This was also in Chicago, and the date was in the spring of 1927 at the Studebaker Theatre. The play was LET US BE GAY, another play by Rachael Crothers who seemed to know just how to write the best drawing-room comedies of this day and era. She also knew how to write the type of roles which fit Miss Larrimore. Here she was in the problems of a divorce, and all of the consequences which are bound to follow. All of these problems were eventually solved, and the wife and her husband were reunited. This was a pattern for a Rachael Crothers play. It was cleverly written, and it was a most amusing evening in the theatre. With her were an accomplished cast which included Barry O'Neil and

Charlotte Granville.

    I am sorry that I missed her in her last show, BRIEF MOMENT, in which she appeared only in New York. This came several years later, and the reviews that I have read state that she had lost none of her special charm and that she had become a very fine actress.

CHARLES LAUGHTON

The death of Charles Laughton in 1967 closed the career of one of our very best character actors. Although I had seen him many times in the films, I only saw him once on the stage.

This event took place on 30 November, 1951, at the Wilson Auditorium of the University of Cincinnati. The play was a revival of DON JUAN IN HELL. This is a part of Bernard Shaw's MAN AND SUPERMAN which has rarely been done in our theatre. The play was done as a reading piece, with the actors at music stands on the stage. It was done in modern evening dress and there was no attempt made to stage the performance at all. It was a new and unique way to do a play, and it was quite an innovation at that time. As the Devil, in perfect evening dress, Mr. Laughton was both beguiling and sinister. His wonderful wit and great personal charm were at their best. He was brilliantly supported by Agnes Moorhead and Charles Boyer.

Of his many films, I seem to recall best MUTINY ON THE BOUNTY in which his Captain Bligh was outstanding; his Mr. Barrett in THE BARRETTS OF WIMPOLE STREET with Norma Shearer; his wonderful performance with Elsa Lancaster in THE BEACHCOMBER; and his pathetically misguided criminal in PAYMENT DEFERRED.

I regret very much that I did not see his last major performance in New York when he revived Shaw's MAJOR BARBARA. This is one of my favorite plays and I am sure that his performance of Andrew Undershaft must have been one of his best.

GERTRUDE LAWRENCE

How does one write about this great and gifted woman? She had an entire world in her hands, and she was beloved by all who ever saw her. She radiated pure glamour everywhere she went, both on and off the stage. She was not always too well-disciplined, but she could play almost anything. She never attempted Shakespeare, but I am sure that she could have been a very fine Kate in THE TAMING OF THE SHREW, if she had ever desired to play this role.

As a very fortunate college freshman, I was able to see her in 1924, in her first American appearance at the Garrick Theatre in Chicago. This was in September of 1924. The show was CHARLOT'S REVUE. In the cast were also Beatrice Lillie and Jack Buchanan. My memories of this performance are not too clear, but I can recall her singing "Limehouse Blues". This song became a landmark of the 'twenties.

It was fourteen long years before I saw Miss Lawrence again. This was on 28 November, 1938 at the Harris Theatre in Chicago. The play was SUSAN AND GOD. After an off-stage line, when she swept onto the stage as Susan I was completely captivated. I vowed that I would never miss seeing her again, if I could be where she was, in whatever she was playing--a play or a musical. I didn't quite make it, but I did see most of her remaining performances.

I saw her next on 12 October, 1940 at the Taft Theatre in Cincinnati. The play was SKYLARK. Here she was supported by Donald Cook and Glenn Anders. It was a frothy play of business versus marital infidelity. She was gracious, charming, and as exciting as ever.

I next saw Miss Lawrence on 24 April, 1943 at the Broadway Theatre in

New York. This was in LADY IN THE DARK. This was a pure "tour de force" for Miss Lawrence. She did everything--a big dramatic part, lots of dancing, and singing. The song "Jenny" as sung by Gertrude Lawrence was a show stopper. It must have been her most taxing role. I loved it.

By 1945 I was out in the Pacific, on D. E.'s which fortunately returned to Pearl Harbor on schedule, so I was most thrilled and pleased that Gertrude Lawrence was touring the various Navy bases. I saw her at the Roosevelt High School Auditorium in Honolulu, in July of 1945. She was playing Elvira in Noel Coward's BLITHE SPIRIT. And what a Ghost she made! Her performance dripped with sex and she gave it everything she had. Mildred Natwick was still playing the Madame Arcati. I had seen the show before at the Fords' Theatre in Baltimore the previous year. I still think that it is Mr. Coward's best play and its situation is one of the funniest in our modern theatre.

I saw her next as Eliza Doolittle in Bernard Shaw's PYGMALION. This was on 30 December, 1946, at the Selwyn Theatre in Chicago. Her Henry Higgins was Dennis King. Having the childhood and adolescent background of Lambeth, a section of London, her cockney was very authentic. She made the role alive, and full of new and different twists. I recall, especially, a bit of business in the "Tea Scene" in which when discussing "mother's milk" and the biting of the bowl off the spoon, the spoon flew to the floor. Her timing, in picking it up was masterful. I saw it again, on tour, in February, 1947, at the Cox Theatre in Cincinnati. Nothing was changed. She was still wonderful.

Five years went by before I saw Miss Lawrence again. This was, unfortunately, for the last time. It was on 23 July, 1951, at the St.

James Theatre in New York. This was, of course, in THE KING AND I. In this great musical, she gave the most polished and the most disciplined performance of her entire career. She was at the height of her long series of successes. She gave a performance that would thrill any audience. The "Shall We Dance" number will remain in my memory as long as I live. Everything that she did in this performance was memorable. Yul Brenner was her able support; he, too, was excellent.

She died a year later, on 6 September, 1952. This closed the career of a brilliant and talented artist who had much to give and who always gave her best. She will remain in the hearts of all who ever saw her-- the most glamorous of all of our stars.

EVA LE GALLIENNE

My memories of Eva Le Gallienne cover a period of forty-seven years. During those years she grew from a young actress with stardom beckoning, to a great actress whose talent, drive, and persistence made her one of the most vital personages in keeping good theatre alive in the United States. The wide variety of roles that she has played, over the years, gave ample evidence of her ability. Her faith in the theatre and her Civic Repertory Company in New York, along with her abiding love of self-discipline, have made her a legend in her own time. Although born in London, her entire acting career has been in the United States. Whether being the daughter of the famous poet, Richard Le Gallienne, was an advantage or a hindrance in her early career is an unanswered question.

I first saw Eva Le Gallienne on 23 April, 1919, at the Majestic Theatre in Peoria. She was playing a small role in THE OFF CHANCE starring Ethel Barrymore. She was nineteen years old, and she was just beginning her long career. The role was not important, but even in her youth she gave promise.

By the next time that I saw her, on 22 September, 1924, at the Blackstone Theatre in Chicago, she had come a long way, and she had reached the stardom that she had desired for so long. In those five years she had grown in stature, and she was in complete command of leading roles. The play was THE SWAN, Molnar's most amusing and, in many ways, most satisfying comedy (although there are some who think THE PLAY'S THE THING is a better play). Miss Le Gallienne had already appeared in LILIOM, which is his finest play, but, unfortunately, I had not seen her in this. As Princess Alexandra she was regal, mature, and, in a certain sense, very lovely in those early days. At no time in her career was she ever considered a physically beautiful actress. She was ably supported by Basil Rathbone, as Agi, the tutor, and Allison Skipworth as the Countess. It was a beautiful performance in every way. She soon began her long and wonderful series of plays by Ibsen and others, and I was fortunate to see many of them over a period of years.

I saw her next on 29 March, 1933, nearly ten years later, at the New Amsterdam Theatre in New York. The play was Chekov's THE CHERRY ORCHARD. In this she played a minor role of Varyna, as Nazimova was the Madame Ravensky. The smouldering frustrations were all there, and they gave evidence of what was to come when she would be playing the major roles in Ibsen's plays.

The next time that I saw Miss Le Gallienne she came on tour with three of the famous plays that she had as her greatest successes at her Civic Repertory Theatre in New York. This was a real example of a true Repertory company, since she played three most varied roles in one week. These were all at the Shubert Theatre in Cincinnati. The first was on 11 December, 1933, when she played THE WHITE QUEEN in ALICE IN WONDERLAND. This was a pure delight for her and for the audience; it was most enjoyable. Josephine Hutchinson was the Alice. On Wednesday, 13 December, I saw her Juliet in ROMEO AND JULIET. While she did not have the passion nor the beauty that Jane Cowl had in the role that I had seen just ten years before, she did have many fine moments of youth and sincerity in this very difficult part. I recall most the Potion Scene, which was moving and beautifully played. Richard Waring was her Romeo. On Saturday night, 16 December, she gave her only performance of HEDDA GABLER. Miss

LeGallienne's was a cold and calculating characterization. Her boredom was evident from her very first entrance. Her sardonic humor in the scene with Judge Brack was a highlight in this performance. The rest of the cast were not quite up to Ibsen, and therefore the production was somewhat uneven.

The next time that I saw her was on 21 February, 1935, again at the Shubert Theatre in Cincinnati. This time she was in L'AIGLON. As "The Eaglet" she was at all times visually convincing and often she was very stirring in the role. She was especially fine in the death bed scene where her simplicity and her earnest pathos were at her top notch best.

The next time that I saw her was during the season of 1937-1938, at the Cox Theatre in Cincinnati. The play was Ibsen's THE MASTER BUILDER. In this very moving and unusual play she was completely in control of the Ibsen technique which is really needed to play his characters to their best advantage. As Hilda Wangle, Miss Le Gallienne gave one of her finest performances. She had youth, beauty, and a sense of the unreal. I shall never forget her cry at the end of the play when Solnes has fallen from the church steeple to his death: "My Master Builder!" It was sheer joy of achievement.

I did not see her again until 15 November, 1943, at the National Theatre in Washington, D. C. The play was UNCLE HARRY in which she was again co-starred with Joseph Schildkraut, after many years. This was pure melodrama which was the "sleeper" of the season and was a great success. In fact, it had a longer run than many of her plays in recent years. It was very exciting, and it gave her a chance to act in a new play that was fresh and untried.

I saw her next on 15 December, 1944, at Fords' Theatre in Baltimore. The play was her last revival of Chekov's THE CHERRY ORCHARD. This time she was playing Madame Ravensky and Joseph Schildkraut was the Gaev. Wisely she had waited many years after the great performance of Nazimova in this part before she played the role herself. While she certainly could not equal nor match Nazimova, she did give to this beautiful and haunting play, a fine feeling for the great depth of sadness that the role must have. She was best at the party scene in Act II, when everyone is remembering the past, and each one is trying to recapture something that can never come again. The greatness in this play lies in its hopelessness, and in the final scene, sincere as Miss Le Gallienne was, she didn't quite reach the deep pathos when she says "good bye" to the cherry orchard as you hear the axes in the distance. Nazimova made me cry; Le Gallienne did not. It was a beautifully staged performance, and the sets were outstanding.

It was twenty years before I saw Eva Le Gallienne again. This was on 27 January, 1964, at the Shubert Theatre in Cincinnati. She was now heading the National Repertory Company, and the play was Chekov's THE SEA GULL. Her Irina (Madame Arkadina) was quite a triumph in her later years in the theatre. She brought all of her great talent and her keen understanding to the role. She was cruel and superficial, she was theatrically pathetic with her son after his attempt at suicide. It was one of her best roles. Ironically, the night that I saw her she had just had the news of the death of Joseph Schildkraut. It must have been a great personal as well as a great professional blow to her, since they had been associated for over forty years. Her performance was even greater because of this sorrow. I have always admired Eva Le Gallienne for her integrity and her great love of the theatre. I have admired her, too, because of her wonderful chance to do all of the roles she wanted to do. She is more or less in retirement now, and it is a pleasure, to me, to have seen her so many times.

EUGENIA LEONTOVICH

There were many qualities about Miss Leontovich which made her a very fine actress. She had authority and charm, and because of her background, she had a thorough training in the theatre. She also had a certain accent in her speaking voice which gave her a very winning personality. On the stage she was gracious and very appealing.

I saw Miss Leontovich for the first time during the season of 1928-1929 at the Princess Theatre in Chicago. The play was CANDLELIGHT. Here she was delightful in the role of a sophisticated woman of the world who had to choose between a man her equal, and a servant. It was a very amusing comedy. She was supported by Alan Mowbray and Donald Brian.

The next time that I saw her was on 29 December, 1930, at the National Theatre in New York. The play was GRAND HOTEL. In this episodic melodrama of life in a great hotel in Berlin before the World War (the Adlon, one assumes) she gave one of her finest performances. There was great dignity and pathos, as well as mystery, in her characterization. Henry Hull was excellent as the Baron and Sam Jaffe was prominently cast. On 8 December, 1931, I saw GRAND HOTEL again, this time at the Grand Opera House in Chicago. The cast was the same except Albert Van Decker had replaced Henry Hull as the Baron.

I saw Eugenia Leontovich next on Christmas Eve, 1934, at the Blackstone Theatre in Chicago. The play was a revival of ROMANCE by Edward Sheldon. Because I had never had a chance to see this old romantic play with Doris Keane, I was drawn to the theatre as I was passing through on my way home for the Christmas holidays. While there were moments in this production which were memorable, even though her supporting cast were mediocre, she never gave to me the real glamour of the capricious prima donna. It was a disappointment.

The last time that I saw Miss Leontovich was again during a Christmas week, that of 1937, at the Harris Theatre in Chicago. The play was TOVARICH. This was one of her most famous roles, and one of her best. As the Grand Duchess of all the Russias, masquerading as a servant, she was captivating and enchanting. It was a delightful performance in every way.

Miss Leontovich has had a long and varied career in the American theatre. She has been, at her best, a most accomplished actress.

BEATRICE LILLIE

There are simply no superlatives left to describe the wonder and the greatness of this amazing comedienne. There is something about her which causes laughter the very moment that she appears on a stage. Even the smallest detail of the movement of a hand, the lifting of an eyebrow, and the constant "spoofing" has its own way of winning an audience. Her singing voice could never be classed as great, but no one cares when she sings a song in her own inimitable manner. My memories of Miss Lillie cover a period of over forty years, and I have never missed a chance to see her when one come along.

I have always considered myself fortunate that I had the good sense, at the age of twenty-one, to want to see what CHARLOT'S REVUE was really like. I had read about this English musical, and I was curious. I saw it during the season of 1924, at the Garrick Theatre in Chicago. This show, of course, introduced me to both Beatrice Lillie and Gertrude Lawrence. I have loved both of them ever since.

I saw her next on 9 April, 1928, at the Illinois Theatre in Chicago. This was in SHE'S MY BABY, a somewhat contrived little show but it did have its moments, and Miss Lillie's singing was much more pronounced than before. There is one memory of her sitting at a table at a fashionable restaurant, fanning herself with a huge stalk of celery. It brought gales of laughter. She was ably supported by Clifton Webb and Jack Whiting.

The next time that I saw Miss Lillie was on 29 June, 1931, at the Music Box Theatre in New York. This was in THE THIRD LITTLE SHOW. Her support here was Ernest Truex, a wonderful comedian in his own right. In this show she sang two of her most popular numbers which have remained famous and memorable throughout her career. One of these was "Mad Dogs and Englishmen", written by Noel Coward for her, which she sang in the full regalia of a British explorer. The second was "There Are Fairies at the Bottom of My Garden" in which she came before the curtain in full evening dress, tiara and all, giving the impression of complete elegance. (Incidentally, this little song had been in the repertoire of Galli Curci when I heard her sing for the first time in the late 'teens, and it was sung then as a straight encore number.) Miss Lillie changed the tempo, and her constant innuendo made it a hilarious caricature of the original. It has remained one of her most popular numbers.

The next time that I saw Miss Lillie she had become "legit" or as she expressed it: "I have become gilded by the Theatre Guild". This was on 28 March, 1932, at the Grand Theatre in Cincinnati. The play was George Bernard Shaw's TOO TRUE TO BE GOOD. It was minor Shaw, but it had moments of his usual wit and caustic satire. Miss Lillie appeared as the Nurse, and the pantomime and the simple hand gestures were outstanding moments to remember in this show. Everyone in the cast was funny. Her supporting cast included Hope Williams, Hugh Sinclair, and Leo G. Carroll. Miss Lillie seemed to float about with no real purpose. It was no doubt an enjoyable experience for her, but she was completely out of her usual element.

I saw her next, during Christmas week of the season of 1935, at the Winter Garden Theatre in New York. The musical was AT HOME ABROAD. She had a great cast with her, including Ethel Waters, Herb Williams, Eleanor Powell, and Reginald Gardiner. One of the big hits of the show was "Double Damask Dinner Napkins" with Mr. Gardiner. This was a complete riot. Miss Waters' songs were electric, and Miss Powell's dancing was outstanding, also.

I saw Miss Lillie next on 13 March, 1937, again at the Winter Garden Theatre in New York. This time the musical was THE SHOW IS ON. Her co-star was Bert Lahr. Among the many amusing moments was the one in which she was in a swing, out over the audience, throwing garters to the assembled crowd. Mr. Lahr was impressive in "Woodman, Spare That Tree" which was a very funny number.

Twelve years passed before I saw Beatrice Lillie again. This was on 2 May, 1949, at the Taft Theatre in Cincinnati, her first Cincinnati appearance in a musical. The show was INSIDE U.S.A. Her co-star was Jack Haley, whom I had seen over twenty-five years before as a blue-eyed young actor in GOOD NEWS. The show was a revue of various areas of the country with special attention to certain places. The big number was "Come, Oh Come, To Pittsburg", which was done with an a capella choir, and it was a minor sensation.

Next comes 1953, in which she had her own show, appropriately titled AN EVENING WITH BEATRICE LILLIE. I saw it for the first time on 23 November, 1953, at the Cox Theatre in Cincinnati, and again on 27 December, 1953, at The Blackstone Theatre in Chicago. Both times she was at her very best, and she sang many of the songs that she had made famous through the years of her long career in the United States. Most memorable were: "The Zither Song", "Maude", "Weary of it All", and, of course, "There Are Fairies at the Bottom of My Garden". In each performance, as I recall now, we had a large theatre party of friends who were all enjoying Miss Lillie as much as we were. Somehow we had the impression that she saw our row, even in the balcony, and that she was singing just for us. Wishful thinking, perhaps, but fun for us.

Nine years went by again before I saw Miss Lillie. This time it was on 6 July, 1964, at the Alvin Theatre in New York. The show was a musical written from Noel Coward's best farce, BLITHE SPIRIT. It was called HIGH SPIRITS. While it was a somewhat average musical with little merit, it did have Beatrice Lillie playing the role of Madame Arcati, and carrying on in her usual manner. She completely saved the show. Her entrance on a bicycle was enough to send the audience into gales of laughter. Tammy Grimes was her co-star as Elvira, and she gave much evidence of her peculiar charm and talent, also.

The few films that Miss Lillie has been in have been landmarks of her special type of humor. One, in which she was co-starred with Bing Crosby, comes to mind. In this she repeated the famous "Double Damask Dinner Napkins", again with Reginald Gardiner. I seem to recall, also, an old movie called ON APPROVAL in which she was very funny. At this writing she is to be in a new film with Julie Andrews and Carol Channing that I shall not miss.

In my opinion, no one in our present day theatre can match Beatrice Lillie as the mistress of pure enjoyment and comedy. She stands alone, and she has no equal.

PAULINE LORD

Pauline Lord possessed one of the greatest talents in the American theatre. In her early years, she was outstanding in a certain type of role and at this time there was no one who could reach the heights that she had achieved. She was alone in her art. As the years went by, this talent never dimmed; but Miss Lord became discouraged because of the parts that she was playing, and this somehow caused her to lose faith in the theatre.

I saw Miss Lord for the first time during the season of 1922-1923, at the Cort Theatre in Chicago. The play was Eugene O'Neill's ANNA CHRISTIE. This role was one of the first to bring her fame. Her Anna was unique. It had the harshness of the woman of the streets; it had, also, a certain quality of pathos and resignation. It was a very great achievement.

The next time that I saw her was in the all-star revival of SHE STOOPS TO CONQUER, at the Blackstone Theatre in Chicago. This was the season 1923-1924. All that she had to do here was to recite the Prologue before the curtain, in this familiar classic. She did a fine job, quiet, and very unassuming.

I did not see her again, until seven years later. This was on 20 January, 1931 at the Grand Theatre in Cincinnati. Now she was cast as Nina in Eugene O'Neill's STRANGE INTERLUDE. This was in the National Company of this famous play. It was a great challenge to follow Lynn Fontanne in this role. However, she gave a brilliant and convincing performance. The compassion and the vague quality that was peculiarly hers, was very evident in this performance. She was always the master of the situation and the role was one of her greatest. Her three men were Ralph Morgan, Donald McDonald, and Harry Bannister. Each in his own way gave the support that was needed, for the role in which each played. It was a milestone in our theatre.

It was fifteen years before I saw Miss Lord again. This was, unfortunately, for the last time. She was now in the road company of Tennessee Williams' THE GLASS MENAGERIE playing Amanda Wingfield. This, again, was a great challenge. To follow Laurette Taylor in the role was something any actress would consider many times before they finally decided to accept the part. The date was in October, 1946, at the Cox Theatre in Cincinnati. I had seen Miss Taylor in the role and I was drawn to the theatre for two reasons: one, I loved the play; two, because I admired Pauline Lord and I wanted to see her again. Miss Lord was not well, and she was not at her best. There were long passages in the play in which she seemed to be completely removed from the character she was playing; however, there were precious moments in which she was completely aware of the role, and in which she gave a poignant and touching performance. The performance was uneven, but I wouldn't have missed it for anything in the world.

My greatest regret is that I was never able to see her Zenobia in ETHAN FROME. I am sure that this must have been her greatest performance in our theatre.

Her death on 11 October, 1950, closed the career of a very great actress. She had been ill a long time, and her resistance finally gave out. We shall miss her.

THE LUNTS

In writing about the most famous couple in the American theatre, I must realize that I saw Alfred Lunt for the first time during the season of 1922 at the Powers Theatre in Chicago. He was playing in support of Billie Burke in THE INTIMATE STRANGERS. In this play he showed a great deal of charm, and a great ability which came into focus in the many roles in which he appeared later. I never saw Miss Fontanne in any of her earlier roles so that I awaited their appearances together with a great deal of interest. For the next thirty-five years, I saw them in the majority of their best performances. There has always been something about their wonderful timing, and their ability to give to each other, so that their performances have consistently been something to watch, to cherish, and to admire.

The thrill of seeing them together came to me for the first time on 27 October, 1930, when I saw them in Maxwell Anderson's ELIZABETH THE QUEEN at the Grand Theatre in Cincinnati. As the aging Elizabeth, Miss Fontanne was at the height of her career. It was a carefully planned and executed performance. She was all that any one could wish in this very demanding role. Mr. Lunt, as Essex, had the virility, the power, and a keen sense of knowledgeability to create his role with ease and near perfection. It remains an exciting memory in my theatrical experience.

The next time that I saw them was on 22 October, 1931, again at the Grand Theatre in Cincinnati. This time they were having one of their many holidays from serious drama. The play was Robert Sherwood's REUNION IN VIENNA, a delightful bit of nonsense about the meeting of two old lovers in Vienna, after many events had transpired in the years between. They had with them a wonderful supporting cast which included Henry Travers, Helen Westley, and Lloyd Nolan. It was a fine comedy and it will remain as one of their best.

I saw them next at the Hanna Theatre in Cleveland. They were still on their holiday. This was in the opening performance, on 28 December, 1933, of Noel Coward's DESIGN FOR LIVING. Noel Coward was with them as the third angle of the triangle. The performance was pure joy from start to finish, and it lasted until long after midnight. Much cutting took place before it opened in New York to rave reviews. The three of them, who represented this amoral triangle, were at their best in a modern comedy of manners. It was pure farce, and each in his own way gave an hysterical performance.

The next time that I saw the Lunts, they had decided to try Shakespeare. They chose THE TAMING OF THE SHREW. I saw it on 29 April, 1935, at the Cox Theatre in Cincinnati. As a production it was full of excitement and at times it was pure "ham". There were great departures from the original text. As Katherine, Miss Fontanne was enjoying a great field day. As Petruchio, Mr. Lunt was having a loud and boisterous romp. They had a wonderful supporting cast with them which included Dorothy Mathews, Sydney Greenstreet, Edith King and Richard Worf. The entire production was geared to the box office and Mr. Shakespeare was sadly missing; but it was great fun, nevertheless.

I saw them next on 29 June, 1936, at the Shubert Theatre in New York. The play was Robert Sherwood's IDIOT'S DELIGHT. Now they were back in the type of role that they do best, the modern, sophisticated, worldly kind of character in which no other actors can match them. It was a heartbreaking play in many ways, showing the futility of all wars. It was staged with excitement and with a sure sense of melodrama, but it carried a great message to all, in a very confused world. Sydney Greenstreet and Richard Worf were prominent in the cast and they were both excellent. In a moment of forced gaiety, Mr. Lunt was very amusing as he danced along with his bevy of girls. Miss Fontanne was excellent, too, as Irene, a woman with a past and a very questionable future.

The next time that I saw the Lunts was in the spring of 1938, at the Erlanger Theatre in Chicago. They were now delving into ancient Greek drama. Their performance in AMPHITRYON '38 was a delight from beginning to end. It was very modern twentieth century Greek farce, but it was done with great finesse and understanding. It was pure entertainment.

I saw them again the following year, when they were on tour in the spring of 1939, at the Taft Theatre in Cincinnati. The play was a revival of Chekhov's THE SEA GULL. Mr. Lunt's Trigorin was full of understanding and he played it with a sureness of touch, as well as with all of the greatness that the role possesses. Miss Fontanne's Irina was not as successful. She was by no means the equal of Edith Evans in this role. Somehow she played only the surface qualities of this very confused woman. She was never very real, and it was a disappointing performance on the whole. The production was noteworthy also, because it brought the young Uta Hagen to the limelight. As Nina, she was making her first appearance in a major role. She was a sensation. From this role she climbed steadily to become the fine actress that she is today.

The pre-dawn of the Second World War was beautifully captured by Robert Sherwood in THERE SHALL BE NO NIGHT. I saw the Lunts next, in this great drama, in the summer of 1939 at the Plymouth Theatre in New York. Gone was the foolishness of past productions, and in this play they were both at their very best. Because of the timeliness and the greatness of the script, they were able to give one of their most memorable performances. (It was not until twenty years later that they found a play in which they could give a performance that matched this one.) The play was propaganda, if you wish, but it was still great theatre. Montgomery Clift and Sydney Greenstreet gave excellent support.

I saw them next on 1 October, 1942, at the Taft Theatre in Cincinnati. The play was THE PIRATE. This was escapist drama, about which I remember very little. I was on leave from the Navy and I picked up the performance while I was home. It was a rather silly play, and added very little to their stature. Estelle Winwood was in the company.

Five years went by before I saw them again. They had been playing THERE SHALL BE NO NIGHT in London, and in many other areas of the "free world", so that their desire to play a comedy again was very understandable. They chose Terrence Rattigan's O MISTRESS MINE, which they played in London and New York to great acclaim. I finally saw it on 21 December, 1947, at the Selwyn Theatre in Chicago. While this play was also escapist, on the age old theme of infidelity, it did have its merits. It was human and it was very real. They were both very fine, and they introduced Dickie Van Patten to the theatre. He was excellent, too.

I did not see them again until 22 January, 1951, at the Taft Theatre in Cincinnati. The play was I KNOW MY LOVE. This was a rather poor play in which they were an old couple on their fiftieth wedding anniversary, recalling their former life. The idea was pleasing, but the play was mediocre.

Another four years went by before I saw the two of them again. This time it was at the Coronet Theatre in New York on 5 March, 1955. The play was Noel Coward's QUADRILLE which he had written especially for them. While this is not one of Mr. Coward's best plays, it does have style. It was so beautifully staged, and so beautifully played, that one easily forgave its many shortcomings. The Lunts were again in their element in this costume piece. Edna Best and Brian Ahern gave them excellent support.

A year later I saw them again, on 23 November, 1956, at the Shubert Theatre in Cincinnati. This was in THE GREAT SEBASTIANS. Here, again, they were in a mediocre play, but they were enjoying every moment of it, and it was great entertainment, if little else.

Fortunately, the last time that I saw the Lunts, they were back in their old groove, giving vital and real performances in a play that was worthy of their talents. I saw them in THE VISIT on 2 November, 1959, at the Shubert Theatre in Cincinnati. Their performance in this tragic and very provocative play was equal to anything that they have ever done on our stage. Together, in one moment, when they recreated their youth and their lost love, they gave one of the finest performances I have ever seen anywhere. Nothing Miss Fontanne has ever done can equal the cruel, sadistic woman she created here. Nor can Mr. Lunt ever hope to equal the tragic overtones that he gave to the pathetic character. Glenn Anders must be remembered, too, in one of the finest performances he has ever given. It was a milestone in modern theatre. It still haunts me.

The Lunts are an American institution. They have no equal in our theatre. Their one film appearance in THE GUARDSMAN was great fun, for those of us who did not happen to see them do it on the stage. Films are never really quite the same, but we were given a rare treat, nevertheless. Their T. V. appearances have been equally rare. One remembers especially THE MAGNIFICENT YANKEE. Here they had wonderful roles to create, and they were both at their best. This was lucky for the many people who were never able to see them on the stage; it was a great pleasure for the rest of us, too, who have seen and loved them for thirty-five years.

VIVIAN MARTIN

Vivian Martin had long been one of the most popular and most vivacious stars of the silent films when she decided to return to the legitimate theatre. She had a wide and faithful following so that this return to the stage was greeted with wide acclaim. It also gave pleasure to those who wanted to see her "in the flesh". I admit that I was one of those faithful admirers, and I was drawn to the theatre for the same reason as many others.

This event took place for me on 26 June, 1922, at the La Salle Theatre in Chicago. The play was JUST MARRIED, a mere trifle as a play--a bedroom farce so popular during this period. It told a story of two honeymooners on a cruise ship who had great difficulty being by themselves. Lynne Overman was her leading man. It had a long run because it was daring and sexy. However, as I look back now, forty-odd years later, I recall very little of this show. I do remember that it was very funny and I did see Vivian Martin.

I recall, also, that her return to the stage was very brief, and that she somehow just seemed to disappear from our midst.

RAYMOND MASSEY

This powerful and truly great actor has had a long and varied career in our theatre. He created the role of Abe Lincoln so brilliantly that he is often identified with that great man while his other fine roles are almost ignored. Before Lincoln he appeared as ETHAN FROMME in a performance that must have been one of the highlights of his career. I did not see this performance, much to my regret.

I saw Mr. Massey for the first time on 20 June, 1939, at the Plymouth Theatre in New York. The play was Robert Sherwood's ABE LINCOLN IN ILLINOIS. His understanding of the greatness and the humility of Lincoln made this one of the landmarks in our theatre. He was eloquent, he was humane, and he was tremendously moving. I shall never forget the scene on the prairie when the small child dies in a covered wagon, nor the election night scene when he quarreled so bitterly with Mary Todd Lincoln, nor the final scene at the station in Springfield, Illinois. In each of these scenes, and in others, he reached true greatness. Adele Longmire was lovely as Ann Rutledge, and Muriel Kirkland was equally fine as Mary Todd Lincoln.

I saw Raymond Massey next on 12 February, 1944, at the Plymouth Theatre in New York. Here he had left the Lincoln legend long enough to appear with Katharine Cornell in Dodie Smith's LOVERS AND FRIENDS. He was now back in a purely romantic role as a soldier in the First World War who was torn between his attachment to his wife and a new romance with a younger woman. He repented, as the play progressed, and returned to his wife. This was not a great play, but it was entertaining, and Mr. Massey gave it stature and dignity. Ann Burr was the younger woman, and she had great charm and promise.

The next two times that I saw Mr. Massey he was again appearing as Abe Lincoln, but in two period of his life quite different from those he had portrayed in the Sherwood play. The first was on 14 January, 1953, at the Taft Theatre in Cincinnati. The play was the very beautiful dramatization of Benet's JOHN BROWN'S BODY. It was not really a play in that it had no plot nor climax; rather, it was a series of episodes from this great poem. As the older and frustrated president who was suffering through the Civil War, he was equally moving and very fine. Tyrone Power, Jr. and Judith Anderson were in the cast. All three of them helped to create much of the beauty of the poetry of this epic. It was a landmark in our theatre.

I saw Mr. Massey for the last time on 22 November, 1957, again at the Taft Theatre in Cincinnati. This was in THE RIVALRY. Here the focus was on the earlier Lincoln. The main purpose of this play was on the Lincoln-Douglas debates in various areas of the middle west. It was a very well-written show piece, and it had a fine sense of drama throughout. Agnes Moorhead and Martin Gabel comprised the remaining cast of three.

My own personal thrill involving Raymond Massey came in November, 1954. He was to be the guest speaker at my church, Christ Church, Cincinnati. Here he delivered a very moving and thought-provoking address. I was fortunate to meet him afterwards, and to have a most pleasant conversation. At this time I was directing a performance of ABE LINCOLN IN ILLINOIS myself, and he gave me most valuable and helpful advice. Later, on the opening night of my performance, he sent a very beautiful letter (which I have kept as a treasured memory) to my amateur cast of high school students. Needless to say, this letter gave my young actors a great feeling of confidence.

CYRIL MAUDE

Mr. Maude had had a long career in the London theatre before he appeared in the United States. He was known for the type of British gentleman who played this kind of role to perfection. He had a suave and urbane manner which in some ways made him a typed actor. His roles were all written for him, and they were patterned to fit his special talent. In many ways he was an English John Drew.

I saw him only once, on 20 August, 1923, at the Gaiety Theatre in New York. The play, AREN'T WE ALL, was an amusing British farce in which he was cast in his usual role. And as the title states, we are all fools to some extent when we try to become a matchmaker. In this he was ably supported by Alma Tell and Leslie Howard as the young lovers.

HELEN MENKEN

When I read, in the summer of 1966, of the death of Helen Menken I was reminded of the many times in the old days that I had seen her. She had ever been one of our most elusive actresses. After retirement, I read about her from time to time; but, aside from her being on various theatrical boards, one heard very little about her. There always was a sharp, somewhat austere, beauty about her, and when she was in her best years she gave many very moving performances. In the four times that I saw her, over a period of years, I recall that in each role there was a simplicity and a sure knowledge of her craft which made her outstanding.

I saw her for the first time in one of her most famous roles, one in which she played for a long run. This was on 20 August, 1923 at the Booth Theatre in New York. The play was SEVENTH HEAVEN. Here, as the slum waif, Diane, she was appealing and very winning. "Heaven" was a simple lodging in Paris where she was befriended and loved by a sewer man, Chico. It was, on looking back, overly sentimental, but at nineteen, on my first trip to New York, I loved it. George Gaul was the Chico. (It served, some years later, as a very famous film with Janet Gaynor.)

I next saw Helen Menken on 26 December, 1929, at the Princess Theatre in Chicago. This was in a pre-Broadway performance of THE INFINITE SHOEBLACK. Again she was playing a woman of easy morals and she had the same wistful appeal that I remembered. The play was something of an allegory in which a young student sold his honor by being bribed to trade examination papers so another student might pass. This was, of course, to gain money for the girl he loved. It was in many ways a very fine play, and it was very moving. Leslie Banks was the student, and he was excellent, as always. I have always admired Mr. Banks for his great charm, and his ability to create a sensitive characterization.

I saw her next on 31 March, 1934, at the Alvin Theatre in New York. This was in MARY OF SCOTLAND, in which she was co-starred with Helen Hayes. There has been much critical opinion about her performance as Queen Elizabeth. However, as I have stated before, while she was not as coldly calculating as Pauline Frederick was in this role, she was very much the autocrat. She was also very queenly and reserved, as Elizabeth was supposed to be.

I saw Helen Menken for the last time on 3 December, 1935, at the Cox Theatre in Cincinnati. This was in THE OLD MAID, in which she was co-starred with Judith Anderson. In my opinion this was her greatest role. As the "old maid" she seemed to live the part and her characterization had warmth, humility, and pathos.

I have always been sorry that she retired from the stage at so early an age. She was a very sensitive and accomplished actress.

Miss Menken died in the summer of 1966.

PHILIP MERRIVALE

Philip Merrivale was one of the most sought-after actors over a period of many years. He came from England at an early age, and established himself in the American theatre. His long career in the United States showed him to be most versatile in a variety of roles. To each he brought a certain sense of the romantic, but he was never considered a matinee idol. He had a quality of being somewhat aloof, but this did not affect his ability as a sensitive performer.

I saw him first during the season of 1917 at the Majestic Theatre in Peoria. The play was POLLYANNA, starring Patricia Collinge. In this he played the role of John Pendleton, the older man who befriends the young girl. It was a purely sentimental play, written from the famous story by Eleanor H. Porter. It hardly added to his stature as an actor, but it served to introduce him to America.

Thirteen years passed before I saw him again. This was on 24 November, 1930, at the Harris Theatre in Chicago. The play was DEATH TAKES A HOLIDAY. This was one of his most famous roles and he played it with wisdom and understanding. Helen Vinson was the Gracia. It was a very beautiful play.

I saw Mr. Merrivale next on 30 October, 1932, at the Shubert Theatre in Cincinnati. The play was CYNARA. This, too, was one of his most famous and successful plays. He played the role here of a somewhat confused man who could not help his attraction for a younger girl whose adoration for him only brought her grief. Phoebe Foster was with him in this play.

When I next saw him it was at the Alvin Theatre in New York. The date was 31 March, 1934. This was in his outstanding performance as Bothwell in MARY OF SCOTLAND with Helen Hayes as Mary, Queen of Scots. His performance was just right for this famous character--he was virile and very exciting. He was Bothwell every moment that he was on the stage. I saw him again on 22 March, 1935 in the same role at the Cox Theatre in Cincinnati. He was just as great as he had been the year before.

Seven years went by before I saw Philip Merrivale for the last time. This was on 26 February, 1942, again at the Cox Theatre in Cincinnati. The play was ROSE BURKE. Here he was co-starred with Katharine Cornell. The play also introduced Jean Pierre Aumont to the United States. It was a contrived melodrama which even the great talents of these stars could not save. The love scene between two middle-aged people (Merrivale and Cornell) was played with good taste and composure, but even so they seemed to be dreadfully embarrassed. This was a pre-Broadway tour, and the play's life in New York was very brief.

Mr. Merrivale had great talent and he will be sorely missed. He died on 14 March, 1946. He is now succeeded by his son, John Merrivale, who is doing quite well for himself both in the United States and in London.

MARILYN MILLER

How does one explain a moonbeam? How can one tell of the elusive quality which Marilyn Miller had throughout her brief career. It is obvious that I have no words to express my fascination and my admiration for this actress. She was quite alone in her own peculiar talent in this century and no one has ever been able to cast the spell that she was able to do merely by appearing on a stage. Her youthful grace, her gracious smile, her childlike beauty, and her perfectly formed body seemed to glide through the air, as if she were on some secluded wires. She had appeal for all ages.

I first saw Marilyn Miller during Christmas week of 1921, at the Colonial Theatre in Chicago. The play was, of course, SALLY. Leon Errol was with her, and even today, over forty-five years later, the memory of that performance has never really dimmed. To me she was the greatest entertainer I had ever seen. (I was eighteen years old.) It is no wonder that the song with Errol, "Look For the Silver Lining", has become a classic tune in the musical comedy field.

I saw her next, again in Chicago, at the Illinois Theatre, on 11 April, 1927. This time it was in SUNNY, with Jack Donahue and Clifton Webb. I have already mentioned my admiration for Mr. Donahue, and their dances together were most outstanding. She seemed simply to float on to the stage. Her dancing always had a special quality, all its own. The hit song was "Who", and it has become famous throughout the years.

Two years later I saw her again, at the Grand Theatre in Cincinnati. The date was 14 January, 1929. This time the play was ROSALIE. Again Jack Donahue was her leading man. Frank Morgan was the comedy lead. How fine he was, too! She danced as blithely as ever with her accustomed grace, but the show was not, as a whole, quite up to either SALLY or SUNNY.

I saw Marilyn Miller for the last time on 30 March, 1934, at the Music Box Theatre in New York. This was in AS THOUSANDS CHEER. It was a star spangled revue with Ethel Waters, Clifton Webb, and Helen Broderick. This was in many ways a most memorable experience. The "Easter Parade" number with Clifton Webb in all of its sepia colors of bygone days, was one of the early production numbers. It was quite breathtaking in its beauty. She had grown greatly, too, as an actress and her mimicry of various actresses of the day was quite clever as well as amazing. She danced divinely, as always.

Her death on 7 April, 1936, just two years later, was a great tragedy. She was so young, so vital, and so much a part of the American scene, that those of us who were fortunate enough to have seen her at her best can never really forget her.

FRANK MORGAN

With his childishly high-pitched voice and his wonderful sense of comedy, Mr. Morgan has long been one of our most accomplished comedians. I have admired him for many years and each time that I have seen him he has been most amusing and completely entertaining.

I saw him for the first time on 6 June, 1926, at the Selwyn Theatre in Chicago. The play was GENTLEMEN PREFER BLONDES. In this marvelous spoof of the "twenties" he was co-starred with June Walker. As the perfect gentleman from Philadelphia he was a pure delight.

I saw Mr. Morgan next as the comedy lead with Marilyn Miller at the Grand Theatre in ROSALIE on 14 January, 1929. He was outstanding, as always.

I saw him next on 8 December, 1930, at the Shubert Theatre in Cincinnati. This was in TOPAZE. Here he was again most entertaining, and he gave a polished performance. He was supported by Clarence Derwent and Catherine Willard. It was a fun show.

Fortunately his movies have been equally entertaining and I recall with pleasure the Saroyan film THE HAPPY PEOPLE and of course, THE WIZARD OF OZ.

HELEN MORGAN

I seem to remember Helen Morgan best as she sat on the piano and sang "Bill" in her plaintive and unique way. I saw her only twice, and both times it was in the same musical, SHOW BOAT. In each she was the Julie that one dreamed of in the novel and in the play.

The first time was on 24 February, 1932, at the Casino Theatre in New York. This was in one of the all-star revivals of SHOW BOAT. Norma Terris, Paul Robeson, Edna May Oliver, Charles Winninger, Dennis King, and Eva Puck and Sammy White were all in this cast. It was a great and memorable evening in the theatre. The entire show was, and still is, perhaps one of our greatest musicals. Musically there are few shows that are filled with such melody, and its story is one that has wide appeal. Miss Morgan "stopped the show" with her great number. There have been many other Julies since then, but none have euqlled her creation of the role. It was always peculiarly hers from the very first.

I saw it again on 5 December, 1932 during its long tour across the country. This was at the Shubert Theatre in Cincinnati. There were many cast changes but Miss Morgan was still on hand, and her talent in this special role had not changed. Norma Terris and Eva Puck and Sammy White were still in the cast, too. In her own way, Helen Margan was one of our most unique performers. She had a certain "lost quality" which came across the footlights in a most appealing manner. She is another actress who cannot be replaced.

CHESTER MORRIS

I first saw Chester Morris when he was just a youngster in his early teens. This was at the Majestic Theatre in Peoria. He was in the cast of THE COPPERHEAD which starred Lionel Barrymore. This was in the season of 1918-19. My memory is dim today of this performance, but I do recall that he was one of the young boys in the early part of the play.

I next saw Mr. Morris about ten years later, during the season of 1927-28, at the Illinois Theatre in Chicago. By now he was an important leading man. He was appearing in support of Lenore Ulric in LULU BELLE. He had taken over the role of the negro barber, George Randall, which had been played by Henry Hull in New York. He gave a very exciting performance of the lover who was deserted by Lulu Belle. However, he followed her to Paris, where he strangled her when she refused to return with him to the United States.

I didn't see Mr. Morris again until 2 October, 1961. He was on tour, and he came to the Shubert Theatre in Cincinnati. The play was ADVISE AND CONSENT. He was playing the role of Senator Knox (from Illinois). This was a political play which brought out the various problems which confront our legislators in Washington. The plot involves the "past" of one of the senators who is being blackmailed because at one time he was suspected of being a homosexual. It was an exciting and dramatic play, and Mr. Morris was outstanding in the role.

I saw Chester Morris for the last time in September, 1966, at the Cherry County Playhouse in Traverse City, Michigan. The play was THE SUBJECT WAS ROSES. This was a Pulitzer Prize play, and it had a long and varied career. Mr. Morris played the role of the somewhat confused father of a young boy who had recently returned from the war in Asia. He brought to the part all of his excellent talent, and he gave a great performance. I had a job as the box office Treasurer at Cherry County Playhouse during the summers of 1964, 1965, and 1966. Because I had seen Chester Morris when he was very young the producer thought this was excellent publicity, and we had our picture taken together. The picture appeared in the Traverse City newspaper along with an interesting article. Naturally, we became good friends, and I had drinks with him frequently in his hotel room.

Just a year ago, in 1970, he was appearing at Bucks County Playhouse here in Pennsylvania in THE CAINE MUTINY COURT MARTIAL. I had hoped to go up to see him play Captain Queeg; but before I could make it, I read in the New York Times that he had died very suddenly from a heart attack. This was a great shock to me, and I sent a brief note to his wife in New York. I quote from her answer: "Thank you so much for your beautiful letter. Chester had been very ill for the past three years and being the trouper he was he kept going until he didn't have any more strength." Lili Morris.

He was a fine actor and a very charming man.

PAUL MUNI

Mr. Muni came up the hard way from his early days in the Yiddish Theatre to the great actor he became. There was honesty of purpose, there was great understanding and great humility in every role that he played. I saw him only twice on the stage, but each time I was thrilled; and I have never forgotten the great impact that his acting left on me.

I saw him for the first time on 12 March, 1933, at the Shubert Theatre in Cincinnati. The play was COUNSELLOR-AT-LAW by Elmer Rice. This was one of his best roles and as George Simon, the lawyer who had come up the ladder to fame, he was brilliant. He was suave, wary, alert, and clever. His cast included Regina Wallace and Jules Garfinkle (later known as John Garfield).

I saw him next on 10 November, 1939, at the Hartman Theatre in Columbus. This was in a pre-Broadway performance of Maxwell Anderson's KEY LARGO. Here as the young crusader who led a small band of idealists into Loyalist Spain, and left them when he considered the cause lost, he was giving one of his best performances. He was sincere and eloquent. In his cast were two young actors, Uta Hagen and Jose Ferrer. It was a memorable evening in the theatre.

Mr. Muni's performances in Hollywood in the films were landmarks in that medium, also. One is not likely to forget his PASTEUR nor his tremendously moving performance in THE GOOD EARTH, with Luise Rainer.

I wish that I might have seen him in his final performances in the theatre, in INHERIT THE WIND, but I was not in New York when he was playing the role. While Melvyn Douglass was excellent in the role of Drummond when I did see the play, I can imagine how really great Mr. Muni must have been, because it is a role that must have fit his special talents perfectly.

Mr. Muni died in July, 1967. As one of our finest actors he is truly irreplaceable.

NAZIMOVA

How does one find words which will convey the dynamic and electric spark that was ever-present in Mme. Nazimova's acting? She had a touch of greatness about her that made her every appearance a very rare experience.

As a child, at home in Peoria, I had seen her many times in the long series of exotic films which she made from about 1918 to the early twenties. Most of the titles of these films escape me now, but I do recall one: BELLA DONNA. In this she was the sultry siren, as usual. These films were, of course, during the silent film era and she had no need to know the English language. However, she did master our language, albeit with a wonderful accent which remained with her always. It was there a great deal when I first saw her on the stage.

The event occurred at the Grand Theatre in Cincinnati. The date was 10 November, 1930. The play, A MONTH IN THE COUNTRY. She was supported by Earle Larrimore and Henry Travers. It was a Russian play in which she was at her best. It was a great treat to see her on the stage and I was at once quite enthralled by her exotic beauty which had never been quite so apparent in the films.

I next saw her at the New Amsterdam Theatre in New York, on 29 March, 1933. The play was Chekov's THE CHERRY ORCHARD. Her supporting cast included Eva Le Gallienne and Paul Leyssac. I suppose that Mme. Ravensky is her greatest role. Since this is one of the really great plays of our generation, it was a wonderful experience, for me, to see it for the first time so beautifully played. Her final moments in the end, when you hear the men chopping down the cherry trees, is something that I shall never forget. Then, too, there is that wonderful moment at the party in Act II, when her forced gaiety was heartbreaking.

I next saw Nazimova at the Cox Theatre in Cincinnati on 23 April, 1936. This was in Ibsen's GHOSTS. In this play she was supported by McKay Morris and Harry Ellerbe. Ibsen was an author whose plays she understood, perhaps better than any other actress who played in them (except, of course, Eva Le Gallienne, who is discussed in another essay). Her Mrs. Alving was done with such sureness, such awareness, and such pathos that it, too, will remain in my memory for a long time. Her final scene with Oswald, at the end of the play, was a great moment in acting.

I saw her for the last time at the Erlanger Theatre in Chicago. The date was 2 January, 1937. This was in another Ibsen play, HEDDA GABLER. Again her supporting cast included McKay Morris and Harry Ellerbe. Her Hedda was cruel, cold, and at times almost frightening. I recall, also, how beautifully she costumed it. In this play, more than in any other, her unique beauty was more evident and she gave a wonderful illusion. It was a masterful job of acting and it was wonderfully staged.

I have always been glad that I was able to see her in at least three of her greatest roles. I am sorry that I missed seeing her in MOURNING BECOMES ELECTRA and THE GOOD EARTH. In both of these plays I am sure that she was excellent. As in the case of several other actresses, Nazimova had few equals and she will long be remembered.

Nazimova died in 1968.

MARIE NEY

Marie Ney is a well-known and prominent actress in the British theatre. To the best of my knowledge she has never appeared in the United States. She is rather tall, with light brown hair, and a very lovely speaking voice.

I saw her first on 18 July, 1934, at the Haymarket Theatre in London. The play was Dodie Smith's TOUCH WOOD. The theme of the play, set, as so many of her plays are, in a resort area where all varieties of people seem to go for their holiday, was that if you "touch wood" all will be well. Here it involves a series of near tragedies which do not happen and life goes on in its usual dull, drab fashion, while all of the members of the play have experienced a few moments of make-believe. She was charming and gracious as the wife. She had a wonderful cast with her which included Flora Robson, Ian Hunter, and Dorothy Hyson.

I saw Miss Ney again on 26 June, 1939, at the Queen's Theatre in London. This time she was in LOVE FROM A STRANGER. In this murder mystery drama she was cast as the wife of a psychopathic murderer who was outwitted in the end. In this play, as the girl who marries a man after a very brief courtship, only to find out the type of man she has married, Miss Ney was excellent. It gave her much more scope than the former play. Frank Voesper, who also wrote the play was the husband. Together they gave very creditable performances.

On both occasions I have enjoyed Miss Ney very much. I do not know what she is doing at this writing, as I have not read of her being in any recent plays in London. Perhaps she is in retirement.

ELLIOT NUGENT

During the past few years illness has kept us from seeing Mr. Nugent. At the present time he is, I believe, just finishing a book which he is writing about his years in the theatre. It should be a very interesting one, as he has had a long and valuable career in our theatre. In his very quiet and unassuming way, he is a remarkably fine actor. My memories of Elliot Nugent cover a period of over forty years.

I saw him first on 25 October, 1919, at the Majestic Theatre in Peoria. The play was TILLIE, starring Patricia Collinge. He was playing a very small role, as one of the neighborhood boys in the Mennonite country. I noted then that he had promise. He must have been very young at the time.

I saw him next on 29 August, 1926, at the Cort Theatre in Chicago. By now, he was a star in his own right. The play was THE POOR NUT. This was one of his most famous roles, and he was a great success. As the frustrated college track star, he was human and very believeable, and he had a very winning personality. In the supporting cast one finds Larry Fletcher, Betty Garde, and Norma Lee. The latter, in private life, was Mrs. Nugent.

It was fourteen years before I saw him again. This time it was on 9 September, 1940, at the Selwyn Theatre, again in Chicago. The play was THE MALE ANIMAL. This wonderful play, with its overtones of James Thurber, gave him a chance to give one of his very best performances. Here, as the college professor who dared to teach the truth of the Sacco Vanzetti case to his students in spite of the risk of being fired from the faculty, he was outstanding. In his support we find Leon Ames, and Elizabeth Love.

I saw him next two years later when he was appearing as the co-star with Katharine Hepburn in a pre-Broadway performance of WITHOUT LOVE. This was on 18 May, 1942, at the Taft Theatre in Cincinnati. As the husband, in name only, he gave a winning performance opposite the glamorous Miss Hepburn.

I saw him next, a little over a year later, on 26 December, 1943, at the Morosco Theatre in New York. Now he was co-starred with Margaret Sullavan and Audrey Christie in THE VOICE OF THE TURTLE. John Van Druten wrote this play purely as escapist drama for the war-torn years. There was no reason for its causing some of the critical comment from some of the purists of the period. It was a complete delight, was played with perfect taste, and was wisely directed. Its title, from the Songs of Solomon, sets the pace of the play. Mr. Nugent, as the lonely and disillusioned soldier, was at his best. He had great appeal.

I last saw Mr. Nugent in the revival of THE MALE ANIMAL at the Music Box Theatre in New York on 28 July, 1952, nearly ten years later. In the revival of this very fine play, Mr. Nugent was as excellent as he had been twelve years before. The years had not dimmed the timeliness of the play, and it seemed even more telling than it had been originally. This time he was supported by Martha Scott and Robert Preston.

Yes, I shall want a copy of Mr. Nugent's book.

Since the above sentence was written, I have found a copy of Mr. Nugent's book EVERYTHING LEADING UP TO THE COMEDY. It is very well written and it gives a fine description of his professional as well as his private life. In it he even mentions the early tour in 1919 with

Patricia Collinge, which I saw at the old Majestic Theatre in Peoria on 25 October, 1919. Today, Mr. Nugent is living in retirement in New York.

NANCE O'NEIL

Miss Nance O'Neil had a long and varied career. She was noted as an actress of great sensitivity and of great understanding. She had a resonant, deep, rich voice which could be heard in the top gallery. She had great depth of feeling, and an abounding passion in the roles that she played.

I saw her only once, during the season of 1920, at the Majestic Theatre in Peoria, and, as usual, from the top gallery. The play was THE PASSION FLOWER. This was one of her greatest successes, and she was now touring the country. As Raimunda, she had the fire and excitement of a Spanish girl who had been jilted by her lover and to whom she eventually brought final disgrace. Charles Waldron was the Esteban, her leading man.

She continued to appear in a series of plays during the remainder of the 1920's, and she retired from the stage in the early 1930's. I have always been glad that I saw this great actress at least once.

ELIZABETH PATTERSON

"Miss Patty" died in February, 1966, at the age of eighty. "Miss Patty" was, of course, Elizabeth Patterson. What a long and wonderful career she had. While her death saddened me, I realized that she had given much happiness and pleasure to a great many people. She was one of the most beloved of our character actresses. My own memories of Elizabeth Patterson cover a period of forty-five years.

I saw her for the first time during the season of 1921-1922, at the Powers Theatre in Chicago. She was playing the character role in the Booth Tarkington play THE INTIMATE STRANGERS, which starred Billie Burke. I fell in love with her at once.

I saw her next at the Blackstone Theatre in Chicago, during the next season of 1923-1924. This was in JUST SUPPOSE. This starred Patricia Collinge, and here again she was the member of the older generation, but one from the deep south.

It was in the late twenties and the early thirties that I saw her next, when she was a member of the Stuart Walker Company in Cincinnati. Because I knew many members of the company, and often saw them socially as well as on the stage, I met Miss Patterson many times; it was at this time that I learned to call her "Miss Patty", as she was called by all who knew her. This company was appearing at the Taft Theatre. The plays in which I most remember Elizabeth Patterson were: CHARM on 5 November, 1928, a pleasing comedy with the young Harry Ellerbe and Muriel Kirkland in the cast; MRS. WIGGS OF THE CABBAGE PATCH on 21 November, 1928, in which her Mrs. Wiggs was warm, understanding and lovable.

My last real memory of Miss Patterson was in a revival of George Kelly's THE TORCHBEARERS, on 5 January, 1931. This has long been one of my favorite plays, and the satire on the "early Little Theatres" with their most inadequate directors and casts remains one of the funniest shows of this period. Elizabeth Patterson, of course, played Mrs. Pampinelli, the director, and she gave it more warmth than Allison Skipworth had given it in the original production. She was equally funny in this famous role.

For the past thirty odd years she has been in Hollywood, continuing in the type of roles that she does best. There were occasional trips back to New York to do a play, also. However, I never saw her again. This is much to my regret.

Yes, we shall miss her.

ANN PENNINGTON

Of the many stars who were created and fostered by the great Ziegfield, none danced more brilliantly into popular favor than Ann Pennington. Small of stature, with a piquant and saucy face she was the essence of the early jazz dancers. She had rhythm, and she possessed beautiful legs which were always displayed to her best advantage. She never achieved the greatness of Marilyn Miller, but she had an extremely loyal public who flocked to see her dance.

I saw Miss Pennington for the first time at the Colonial Theatre in Chicago during the season of 1920-1921. She was in the GEORGE WHITE'S SCANDALS. She was young, vivacious, and danced with ease and charm. Mr. White was also in this cast, and so was Lou Holtz.

I saw her next at the New Amsterdam Theatre in New York, on 20 August, 1923. By now she had arrived and she was one of the shining lights in the ZIEGFIELD FOLLIES. Here her dances were given more prominence, and she was winning and delightful.

The next time that I saw her she was back in the Scandals. This was at the Erlanger Theatre in Chicago, on 27 July, 1927. The show was called SCANDALS OF 1927. In her supporting cast were Willie and Eugene Howard, as the comedy team, and Frances Williams as the chief singer. Also, I note that Tom Patricola was in this cast. This was in the mid-twenties, jazz was in full swing, and Ann Pennington's most famous number was "Black Bottom". Of all her dance creations, this one is no doubt her most famous, and the one for which she is most remembered.

Miss Pennington died in November 1971, in New York. She was 77.

OSGOOD PERKINS

Here we have another actor who, in his quiet way, was unique in our roster of American actors. His untimely death, when he was appearing with Gertrude Lawrence in the opening performance of SUSAN AND GOD at the National Theatre in Washington, D. C., closed the career of a really fine actor who was just coming into his own as a star.

I saw Mr. Perkins first on 7 September, 1924 at the Adelphi Theatre in Chicago. The play was BEGGAR ON HORSEBACK. The stars in the play were Roland Young and Spring Byington. It was a very funny farce of the world of business, and Mr. Perkins played the role of Homer Cady, the son. While the role was secondary to Mr. Young and Miss Byington, he made it stand out.

I saw him next at the Shubert Theatre in Cincinnati, nearly ten years later, on 17 October, 1932. The play was THE PURE IN HEART. His supporting cast included June Walker, and Paul Kelly. This was a pre-Broadway tryout, and it was a very confused and poorly written play which lasted only briefly in New York. The entire cast tried valiantly, but there was little to give it much substance.

I saw Mr. Perkins for the last time in the fall of 1936, at the Cox Theatre in Cincinnati, in support of Ina Claire in END OF SUMMER. Here he was at his urbane best and the role was perfect for his peculiar charm. The cast also included Van Hefflin. This was a real play with a real purpose, and Mr. Perkins made his role a memorable one.

Fortunately, for us who love the theatre, his son Anthony Perkins has become one of the finest of our younger actors. He is carrying on the tradition that his father left for him.

TYRONE POWER, JR.

Young Tyrone Power, Jr. skyrocketed to fame very quickly in the films. He was, for several years, a matinee idol, very famous and much admired by a large and adoring public. How much was personality and good looks, and how much was acting talent that he had inherited from his famous father, has always been questionable. I have always taken the middle road as to his talent. He did possess a magnetic personality which was his greatest asset. He appeared on the stage, also, for a limited number of plays.

I saw him for the first time before he had skyrocketed to fame, on Christmas Eve, in 1934, at the Blackstone Theatre in Chicago. It was in a revival of ROMANCE which Eugenie Leontovitch had put together for her own special talents. She discovered that MME. CAVELENI was not her best role, and the show had a somewhat short life. Young Power was cast in a small role as the grandson who is listening to his grandfather tell the story of his youthful "slip from grace" when he was the adored favorite of a famous opera singer. Mr. Power had little to do, so it was unfair to judge his talent.

I didn't see him again until nearly twenty years later. This was on 14 January, 1953, at the Taft Theatre in Cincinnati. Here he was cast, along with Judith Anderson and Raymond Massey, in a dramatization of Stephen Vincent Benet's JOHN BROWN'S BODY which was done as a theatre piece with choral background. He appeared as the young soldier, and while it was a very interesting evening in the theatre, Mr. Power again had very little to do. He was, however, a far more poised and accomplished actor.

I saw him a year later on 3 January, 1955, again at the Taft Theatre in Cincinnati. He was now on a pre-Broadway tour with Katharine Cornell and Christopher Plummer in THE DARK IS LIGHT ENOUGH. Since he was now cast in a much more mature role, also one that was far more convincing, it was much easier to evaluate his talent. He was good in the part, and there were moments in which his great personal charm added to this very confusing play, but they were fleeting. As a whole, one could never consider thae he was any more than a very adequate actor.

His sudden death a few years ago in Rome was a great tragedy to his many admirers. It was a loss, too, to what he might have become in the theatre with work and training.

YVONNE PRINTEMPS

This charming and vivacious French star of the musical comedy stage has had an international reputation. While she is most often seen in Paris, she has appeared in New York and London. She has great vitality, personal charm, and beauty. She seems ageless as she has had a long and varied career.

I saw her first in June, 1934, at His Majesty's Theatre in London. The play was Noel Coward's CONVERSATION PIECE. She was very lovely to see and most pleasing to hear. As Melanie, a young French girl who is taken to England by a Duke to make an advantageous marriage, she "turns the tables" and will have only the Duke. "I'll Follow My Secret Heart" was the most memorable tune. It has a lilting melody and it is still popular today. Pierre Fresnay was the Duke. The staging was quite in keeping with the style of the period.

I saw her only once again. This time it was in July, 1937, at the Theatre Des Bouffes Parisiens in Paris. The play was TROIS VALESE. This was another period play which covered the years, 1867-1900-1937, in which Miss Printemps appeared first as the grandmother, then the mother, and finally as the daughter--all of whom were famous in their day as Cabaret singers. It was beautifully staged and Yvonne Printemps was excellent in all three periods. The charming waltz tune was played throughout, and in the final scene "Je Ne Suis Pas" was the most catchy tune. Here she sang and danced with great abandon, as well as great charm. Pierre Fresnay was again her leading man. In fact, I was so captivated by this show that I went back to see it a second time, and took friends of mine who happened to be in Paris that summer. This brings to mind an amusing memory, too. One of the friends was a teacher of French in an American high school, and she purchased the booklet which had all of the music and the lyrics to use back home in her classes. After careful scrutiny she decided that the lyrics to the "Je Ne Suis Pas" number were a bit too risque for the tender minds of the young, and she had to abandon the idea.

MARJORIE RAMBEAU

As I have already stated in earlier pages, Marjorie Rambeau was one of the three most beautiful women I ever saw on the stage. I saw her only twice, and both times were many years ago, but I still remember the beautiful face and figure of this very charming person.

I saw her first in the season of 1919-1920, at the Majestic Theatre in Peoria. She was on tour in the allegory, EYES OF YOUTH. In this play she appeared in various stages of a woman's life. The play was somewhat like EVERYMAN, and it showed all the pitfalls and the temptations that she mastered along the way. I recall, too, that for those early days it was beautifully staged.

The only other time that I saw Miss Rambeau was on 30 December, 1921, at the La Salle Theatre in Chicago. The play was DADDY'S GONE A-HUNTING. I understand from Mr. Blum's fine record of our greatest actors and actresses, that this was her favorite role. This is easily understood. The play was of a misunderstanding between a husband and wife, and a knowledge of the double standard of infidelity for women as well as for men. It had many overtones of THE SECOND MRS. TANQUERAY, but it could stand on its own merits. She gave to her role of the wife all of her greatest talents, and it was a performance to remember. Her leading man was Frank Conroy.

Of all of the films in which she appeared after she left the stage and went out to Hollywood, only one remains clear in my memory. This was THE PRIMROSE PATH, starring Ginger Rogers and James Stewart. Her role of the mother in this story of three generations of prostitution was beautifully done. It had a warmth of understanding, and she gave to it her own unique quality of being able to rise above the sordidness of the plot and to remain aloof.

Yes, Marjorie Rambeau was an actress one does not easily forget.

Miss Rambeau died at the age of 84 in 1970, in California.

BASIL RATHBONE

Basil Rathbone has had a long and prominent career in our theatre. He was, in his earlier years, a popular leading man in the matinee idol class. He has a dignity of bearing and he is very handsome. However, I have always felt that there was, and still is, a certain coldness in his acting. He has never been able to create any real warmth of characterization in the roles which I have seen him play. Even so, he has always been interesting to watch. Also, he does have a well-modulated speaking voice, and he is noted for his near perfect diction.

I saw Mr. Rathbone for the first time on 22 September, 1924, at the Blackstone Theatre in Chicago. The play was THE SWAN, starring Eva Le Gallienne. As Dr. Agi, the tutor, he gave a very fine performance. He was young then, and he played his scenes with Philip Merrivale, as the Prince, quite brilliantly.

I saw him next on 2 September, 1928, at the Studebaker Theatre in Chicago. The play was THE COMMAND TO LOVE. In this play, which was a delightful bit of nonsense, he appeared as Gaston, a military attache. He was very suave, and the perfect type for this role. He was supported by an all-star cast which included, Mary Nash, Cora Witherspoon, and Ferdinand Gottschalk.

The next time that I saw Basil Rathbone was on 14 May, 1932 at the Selwyn Theatre again in Chicago. The play was THE DEVIL PASSES. In this play as the Rev. Nicholas Lucy he was giving one of his best performances. The role fitted him perfectly as he could be cold and sinister in keeping with the part. He had another all star cast with him this time, too. It included Mary Nash, Cecelia Loftus, Arthur Byron, Robert

Lorraine, and the young and very beautiful Dianna Wynward making her first American appearance.

I didn't see Mr. Rathbone again until the week of 2-7 April, 1934, when he was touring with Katharine Cornell at the Shubert Theatre in Cincinnati. Here he was in all three of the plays that Miss Cornell had in her repertoire that season. First, as Robert Browning in THE BARRETTS OF WIMPOLE STREET, he was good and often played the role very well; however, he lacked the charm that Brian Ahearn had given to the part. As Romeo, in ROMEO AND JULIET, he read the Shakespearean lines with ease and much beauty, but he lacked the romantic intensity of the young lover. As Morrell, in CANDIDA, he again was cold and he seemed to have no sense of humor; in fact, he was often quite dull.

It was fifteen years before I saw him again. This was on 21 February, 1949, at the Cox Theatre in Cincinnati. The play was THE HEIRESS. As Dr. Austin Sloper, Basil Rathbone gave the finest performance I have ever seen him give. The role suited his talents, and he was calculating and diabolical. He was in complete mastery of the part throughout. Beatrice Straight appeared as his daughter, Catherine, and she was excellent. Patricia Collinge was also in the cast. It was great theatre.

The last time that I saw Basil Rathbone was on 22 June, 1957 at the Playhouse in The Park in Philadelphia. The play was THE WITNESS FOR THE PROSECUTION. As Sir Wilfred Robarts, he was very uneven. There were moments when he was excellent, but others when he seemed very insecure. Anne Meachem was the Romaine, and she was outstanding.

Today he is giving lectures throughout our country. Twice he has been in Cincinnati, but I was unable to hear him due to other engagements.

Mr. Rathbone died in the summer of 1967.

FLORENCE REED

Of all of the actresses who appear in these pages, my personal memories of Florence Reed cover a wide period of years, and show her to be one of our most versatile actresses. I have seen her many times in the long period of over fifty years in the theatre. I have seen her in classic melodrama, in Shakespeare, and in outstanding comedy roles. She is a small woman, but because of her innate ability she has always been able to have complete mastery of the stage in whatever role she happened to be appearing. She is also of the old school of wide gestures and a hauntingly mellow voice, a voice that could shake the rafters, if need be, when she chose to use it.

I saw her first at the Illinois Theatre on 26 January, 1924, in Chicago. The play was THE LULLABY. Here she played the role of a misunderstood woman who spent the greater part of her life repenting of things that she had done in yer youth. It was pure melodrama, in which she ran the gamut of all of the emotions. She was unique, and very interesting in this role. It is a very apt commentary that many years later this play was made into a film called THE SIN OF MADELON CLAUDET which gave Helen Hayes her first film appearance. Miss Hayes won an "Oscar" for her performance in this old play.

I saw Florence Reed next three years later, on 8 April, 1927, at the Adelphi Theatre in Chicago. The play was THE SHANGHAI GESTURE. I suppose Mother Goddamn was her most famous role. This melodrama had great appeal because of its theme and its authentic Chinese setting. She was supported by Percy Warm, and Mary Duncan was Poppy, her daughter. It was a great performance.

1929 was a banner year, as I saw her three times in a wide variety of roles. On 18 March she was touring the country, along with William Farnum (of film fame) and Lynn Harding, in MACBETH. It played at the Emery Theatre in Cincinnati. Her Lady Macbeth was the first Shakespearean role in which I ever saw Miss Reed. She was vocal and masterful in the role, but in some instances she did not reach the heights that Judith Anderson did, when I saw her do Lady Macbeth, many years later. The following fall she joined the Stuart Walker Company in Cincinnati for two guest star appearances. This was in a revival of Somerset Maugham's OUR BETTERS. As Pearl Grayson she was excellent in the role of the American woman who had married into English royalty. The pure sham of this very false existence was very brilliantly brought out in this play. I still consider it to be one of Mr. Maugham's best plays, and Miss Reed was just right for the role. Catherine Calhoun-Doucet was also in the cast, as the Duchess, and she was equally fine in her role.

Two weeks later, on 11 November, again at the Taft Theatre, I saw her in another Somerset Maugham play, EAST OF SUEZ. It had all of the clever writing that we expect from Mr. Maugham and while it had, too, all of the mystery of the East, it was not as good a play as the former. Miss Reed, unfortunately, had a tendency to play Mother Goddamn all over again, and this put the entire play out of focus. Russell Hicks was her leading man.

I didn't see her again until 1 February, 1932, when she was on tour with the National Company of Eugene O'Neill's MOURNING BECOMES ELECTRA. She was playing the role of the mother, Christine, which had been created in New York by Nazimova. This was at the Grand Opera House in Cincinnati.

Now she was again at her best, and she gave the role great dignity as well as great fear. She was moving and pathetic. The Lavinia was Judith Anderson, the Orian, Walter Abel, and Crane Wilbur (again out of a long history in silent films) was the Adam Brandt. It was a very thrilling evening in the theatre.

Five years later, I saw Miss Reed again in a comedy role. She was having a "busman's holiday" in this very amusing role. This was at the Cox Theatre on 11 October, 1937. The play was YES, MY DARLING DAUGHTER. I had never seen her before in this type of frothy, light comedy. She was quite amazing in the way that she could play comic as well as the more mature, tragic roles. It was a fun comedy with a great deal to enjoy. In her company were two young actors, Owen Davis, Jr. and Helen Flint, both of whom I had seen some ten or more years before in THE BARKER. It was good to see them again.

The next time that I saw Florence Reed was in Washington, D. C., at the National Theatre on 9 November, 1942. It was the first performance anywhere of Thornton Wilder's THE SKIN OF OUR TEETH. The stars were Tallulah Bankhead, and the Marches (Frederic and Florence Eldridge). Miss Reed played the Fortune Teller in the second act, and her earthy quality was even more present.

I saw her next in a dramatization of Daphne Du Maurier's REBECCA at Fords' Theatre in Baltimore on 2 October, 1944. This was a far cry from the almost perfect film which had been made from this almost perfect story. The play lacked something, and it was never really very exciting, nor was it very interesting. Miss Reed's "Mrs. Danvers" was very well played, but the role was badly written and she had little to do. Dianna Barrymore was woefully miscast as the second Mrs. De Winter, and Bramwell Fletcher was not at his best as De Winter. It was, in reality, a failure.

A year or so later, I saw her again in a Shakespearean role. She was in the pre-Broadway tryouts of THE WINTERS TALE, which I saw on 19 November, 1945, at the Cox Theatre in Cincinnati. This is a play that is rarely done, and the Theatre Guild revival was quite a treat. Her Paulina had fine overtones, and she gave it great dignity and read the lines with tremendous effect. She was far above the rest of the cast, even though it included some very fine actors. These were Henry Daniell and Jessie Royce Landis. Even so, she stood out.

The last time that I saw Florence Reed was on a very hot night on 31 July, 1955, at the Blackstone Theatre in Chicago. This was in the performance done in Paris of Wilder's THE SKIN OF OUR TEETH. This time it starred Helen Hayes and Mary Martin. Miss Reed played her original role of the Fortune Teller, and her characterization had not changed from the original. She was still the master of the situation.

Now that Miss Reed is in retirement, she must have many wonderful memories of her long and varied career. She is an American actress to remember. I feel very fortunate to have seen her so many times.

Florence Reed died on 12 November, 1967, in New York.

JAMES RENNIE

James Rennie has been a popular star for many years. My own memories of him begin over forty years ago. He was, in his youth, a great matinee idol, and he was very engaging in all of the roles that he played. He had great personal charm (he still has this same charm); and while he would never be considered a great actor, he is certainly a most competent and delightful one to watch.

I saw him first on 1 January, 1923, at the Powers Theatre in Chicago. The play was SHORE LEAVE, and he was the leading man with Frances Starr. As the sea going Gob who brings new hope into the life of the spinster seamstress, he was very entertaining.

I saw him next, at the end of the same year, on 16 December, at the Adelphi Theatre in Chicago. The play was THE BEST PEOPLE. The play had a fine satirical theme, and was very well played. As Henry, the chauffeur who marries the daughter of his rich boss, Mr. Rennie was again enjoyable. The cast included Margaret Dale, Frances Howard, and Gavin Muir.

I saw him next on 8 August, 1926, at the Studebaker Theatre, again in Chicago. The play was THE GREAT GATSBY. In this dramatization of F. Scott Fitzgerald's great novel, Mr. Rennie was always in complete control. He had matured into a very fine actor, and he gave to the role everything that it demanded. In fact, this is considered to be his finest role. As the young idealist who gains great wealth through bootlegging, and who is unjustly killed at the end, he played with fine understanding and pathos. Helen Baxter was most appealing as the Daisy Fay.

This was the turning point in Mr. Rennie's career, and he had now very definitely arrived. He was much sought after, as a leading man of prominence and talent. This was increasingly obvious by the next time that I saw him, which was on 5 June, 1933, at the Harris Theatre in Chicago. The play was ALIEN CORN and the star was Katharine Cornell. In this play he played the bigoted business man who was a trustee of the small college situated in a town in Iowa. His role had stature and authority.

I saw him next, twelve years later, on 18 January, 1945, at the Locust Theatre in Philadelphia. The play was the pre-Broadway tryout of ONE MAN SHOW. In this he was again the business tycoon, a type of role which he played best. The play involved an Art Gallery owned by a father and daughter. However, the father's possessiveness of his daughter nearly wrecks her life. Frank Conroy and Constance Cummings were the father and daughter. The play was not a success, but I liked it in spite of the poor reception that it later received in New York.

I saw James Rennie, a little over a year later, on 26 August, 1946, at the Blackstone Theatre in Chicago. The play was THE STATE OF THE UNION. Here once again he had a fine part. In this play, a very human domestic comedy with political overtones, one sensed a love of laughter as well as a love of country. As Spike McManus, he had a field day. The cast included Judith Evelyn and Neil Hamilton (of silent movie fame). It was a most enjoyable evening in the theatre.

The last two times that I saw Mr. Rennie were about two years apart. He was playing the Captain in MISTER ROBERTS, and, incidentally, he was playing it very well. The first time was on 28 December, 1948, at the Erlanger Theatre in Chicago; the second was on 5 December, 1949, at the Taft Theatre in Cincinnati. In both performances John Forsyth was the Mister Roberts.

It has been interesting to see the growth of James Rennie as an actor throughout all of these years.

Mr. Rennie died in the spring of 1967.

PAUL ROBESON

Today, this great star, who has so much talent and who is so outstanding, is quite ill and in retirement. Some of his problem is due to his misguided loyalties to his country, and the fact that, over a period of years, he lived in Russia where, under the Communist regime, he seemed to find solace and comfort only to discover how false it was. This has been a great loss to our theatre, and he was one of our really great actors and singers.

I saw him for the first time in June, 1932, at the Casino Theatre in New York. The play was, of course, SHOW BOAT. As Joe, he was perfectly cast, and he was singing beautifully. No one will ever forget "Old Man River" as Robeson sang it. He brought a joy of living to his role that was engaging. The cast was as nearly perfect as any cast can be. It included Edna May Oliver, Norma Terris, Dennis King and Helen Morgan.

I saw Paul Robeson next on 3 January, 1944, at the Shubert Theatre in New York. The play was OTHELLO. As this tragic character, he gave the finest performance I have ever seen. In every sense he was the Moor beset with overpowering jealousy, and his stature and great dignity gave the role complete balance. He read the Shakespearean lines with great understanding and humility. Uta Hagen, Jose Ferrer, and Margaret Webster (in one of her very rare appearances on the stage) gave him excellent support. Since this was the first performance in which there was a mixed cast, it caused quite a stir, although not nearly as much as had been expected.

I saw him for the last time in March of 1945, at the Geary Theatre in San Francisco. Again, it was in OTHELLO. The long months that he had played the role had in no way dimmed its greatness. The only cast change was Edith King, in the place of Margaret Webster as Emelia.

I repeat, his loss to our theatre is a tragic waste.

MAY ROBSON

May Robson was one of the most beloved of our actresses. She toured for years up and down the entire country. She was one of the old school who thrived on one night stands. She had an infectious humor and a keen knowledge of the theatre, as well as a sure feeling of how to win over an audience. She was a rather large woman, but her size only added to her ability to create the roles for which she was famous. In the early twenties, I was fortunate to see her several times as she always came back each year. I recall, also, that she always played to full houses, as her public was wide and very devoted. In the period between 1920 and 1924 I saw her four times.

I saw her first on 4 November, 1920, at the Majestic Theatre in Peoria. She was appearing in IT PAYS TO SMILE. This was typical of all of her plays. They were pleasing and entertaining, but of no great literary merit. Each one was styled to her own special talents, and the titles were of little importance.

The next time that I saw Miss Robson was during the season of 1921, again at the Majestic Theatre in Peoria. This time it was MOTHER'S MILLIONS. The theme was the same and the part for May Robson had changed little. In each of these plays I note, from my programs, that Russell Hicks was in the cast. I saw him many years later when he was a member of the Stuart Walker Stock Company in Cincinnati.

The next year, on 20 October, 1923, she brought a revival of one of her most famous plays; THE REJUVENATION OF AUNT MARY. It was a huge success all over again, and we all loved her.

The last time that I saw May Robson was on 11 October, 1924, again at the Majestic Theatre in Peoria. This was in TISH made from the amusing stories of Mary Roberts Rinehart. This was perhaps her best play, and the one in which she gave her most to her admiring audience. Over forty years later, I still remember her with much pleasure. She gave laughter, gaiety, and warmth to her characterizations. In her own way she was unique, because no one has ever been able to capture the same sense of comedy that she possessed.

After many years of retirement, she died on 20 October, 1942.

JULIA SANDERSON

My memories of Julia Sanderson go back over many years. I saw her only twice, but each time she had a quality of winsomeness and a peculiar charm that was most engaging. She also had a very sweet and winning voice, which captivated all of her audiences in those bygone years.

I saw her first, during the season of 1915-1916, at the Majestic Theatre in Peoria. I was only a child at the time, but the memory is ever green. The play was THE GIRL FROM UTAH, which I suppose is her greatest single hit. She was supported, even on tour, by Donald Brian and Joseph Cawthorne. It had something to do with the Mormon movement as it was reaching the West, and the fate of a young girl who was torn between the possibilities of being one of several wives or of marrying the man whom she loved. She won out in the end, and married the man of her choice. The hit of the show was, of course, Miss Sanderson's singing of "They Didn't Believe Me". This was a most winning and infectious tune which has somehow survived the years; even today, over fifty years later, one still hears this song from time to time. I am especially happy that I have in my record collection a rare record which includes Miss Sanderson's singing of this song. I play it frequently--and it does bring back fond memories of that night fifty years ago, when I first heard her sing it.

The only other time that I saw Miss Sanderson was ten years later. The date was 16 March, 1925, at the Apollo Theatre in Chicago. The musical was MOONLIGHT. She was now co-starred with Frank Crummit, a very popular singer of the day. Certain tunes remain from this show: "Say It Again", "Old Man in the Moon", and "Don't Put Me Out of Your Heart". She was still very lovely, and a very gracious woman who had never lost that certain quality that made her a lady. In the next few years she was heard frequently with Mr. Crummit over the radio. Here, again, it was a joy to hear her lovely voice. She was a very lovable person, and a great entertainer.

FRITZI SCHEFF

This ex-Metropolitan Opera soubrette, most famous as Musetta in LA BOHEME, and in FIDELIO at the turn of the century, has had a long career in light opera. She quite easily became a legend in her own time--and no one has ever sung "Kiss Me Again" with quite the same abandon, nor, when she was younger, in better voice. In her own way, she was a very unique artist.

My memories of Fritzi Scheff cover a period of forty-seven years. During this time I only saw her twice, and there was a wide span of years in between.

I saw her for the first time on 11 December, 1920, at the Majestic Theatre in Peoria. The play was GLORIANNA. It was a musical made from an older play called A WIDOW BY PROXY. I recall very little of this show, now all of these years later, but my program tells me that she had a place at the end of the show, which was called simply, "Songs". It was then, during this part of the show, that I heard her sing the immortal "Kiss Me Again" for the first time. I do recall how thrilled I was; and I recall, too, the great applause from a sold out "one night stand".

Ten years later I saw her again, on 2 March, 1930, at the Shubert Theatre in Cincinnati. This was in her last revival of MLLE. MODISTE by Victor Herbert. This was the show in which she had won international fame. The years had been kind to her, and her comedy sense was still intact; also, her voice was still big, and she sang the old favorites, "Kiss Me Again", and "Nightingale and the Star", with her old charm and verve. It was a rewarding evening. She came back again in various night clubs in New York, from time to time, but I never saw her again.

Fritzi Scheff held a beloved place in the American theatre; she was a popular singing actress for many years.

VIVIENNE SEGAL

As a star of the musical stage, Miss Segal has had a long and very enviable career. She possesses great beauty and a pleasing, throaty, singing voice. She also has a tremendous sense of theatre. Over the years I have seen her four times.

The first time that I saw Miss Segal was on 13 June, 1926, at the Olympic Theatre in Chicago. The show was CASTLES IN THE AIR. She was ably supported by Bernard Granville and J. Harold Murray. Somehow, I recall very little of this production; it was a blend of musical comedy and operetta, and while it was tuneful, it wasn't memorable.

I saw Vivienne Segal the next time on 4 February, 1929, at the Grand Theatre in Cincinnati. The musical was Ziegfield's THE THREE MUSKETEERS. This told of the famous three who were now having their adventures to music. Dennis King was the D'Artagnan. The songs that were memorable were: "Heart of Mine", "Kiss Before I Go", and Every Little While". These were written and composed by Friml for this show.

I saw her next on 10 January, 1932, at the Grand Theatre in Cincinnati. The show was a revival of THE CHOCOLATE SOLDIER. Charles Purcell was her leading man. Together they were very pleasing in the old melodies, which came across the footlights as if they were new tunes. "My Hero" was, as usual, much applauded.

I did not see Miss Segal again for twenty years. The last time was on 30 July, 1952, at the Broadhurst Theatre in New York. The show was a revival of PAL JOEY. She had also been in the original cast playing the same role. None of her talent had dimmed, nor had her beauty, and she gave one of the finest performances of her career. "Bewitched, Bothered and

Bewildered" was as lovely as ever. Harold Lang was the gigolo, and he sang and danced with fine spirit. It was a wonderful show.

OTIS SKINNER

As I look back over the years, I feel that I was very fortunate to see Otis Skinner so many times. I was fortunate, too, in being able to see him in a wide variety of roles. Of all of the actors of the "old school", I suppose he had more personal charm and more innate acting ability than many others of his period. He had a warmth of personality, and a kindliness of character, that came through to his audiences no matter what role he was playing.

I saw him first on 7 April, 1921, at the Majestic Theatre in Peoria. The play was MISTER ANTONIO. Here he was the lovable organ grinder, who brought cheer and happiness to all around him. He had played the part many times, but there was always something new each time that he played it. It remains a fond memory.

I saw him next, at the Illinois Theatre, in Chicago. The play was BLOOD AND SAND. In this play, he was an older Spanish bull fighter who had seen better days. It was an entertaining play, and held one's interest throughout. The Dona Sol was Catherine Calvert. An interesting point to note here: I find, in looking over the program, that Cornelia Otis Skinner, his daughter, had a small role. This was one of her earliest appearances.

I next saw Otis Skinner on 12 May, 1924, at the Orpheum Theatre in Peoria. This time it was in SANCHO PANZA, a play that had been written from the memoirs of the great Don Quixote. Here he was at his best in a great comedy part, and he brought to the role all of his personal qualities which made him a joy to watch. It was good theatre.

Six years went by before I saw him again. This time it was on 8 March, 1930, at the Grand Opera House in Cincinnati. The play was PAPA

JUAN--also known as A HUNDRED YEARS OLD. There was something very special about this old man who was celebrating his one hundredth birthday with all of his family around him. The small family problems which usually arise were all here, but Otis Skinner seemed able to surmount the bickerings and to have a complete understanding of his relatives. One came away feeling that his life must have been a good one.

Two years later, on 28 January, 1932, I saw Mr. Skinner for the last time. Here, out of loyalty and love of the theatre, he came out of retirement to appear as co-star with Maude Adams in Shakespeare's THE MERCHANT OF VENICE. Shylock was a role that he had played many times before--even so long ago as to have appeared in this role with Ada Rehan. My notes tell me that he wore the same costume in this revival that he had used when he appeared with Miss Rehan. While the entire evening had been geared to the return to the stage of Miss Adams, Mr. Skinner never lost a moment in his wise and thoughtful characterization of Shylock. Perhaps he was more human than some; but he had a great dignity, and he gave the role more sympathy for the man than for the crafty money lender, which has been the characterization of many other actors.

Mr. Skinner died ten years later on 4 January, 1942. He had long been in retirement. His death left a great void in the American theatre. Fortunately his daughter, Cornelia Otis Skinner, has made a great name for herself in her own right. Through her we can always remember her father with affection--but more of her in another essay.

FRANCES STARR

Miss Frances Starr had been one of Belasco's most famous stars for many years before I was able to see her. Because of this, I was always hoping that the time would come when I would have this pleasure.

The time finally arrived. I saw her for the first time on 20 January, 1923, at the Powers Theatre in Chicago. The play was SHORE LEAVE. Her leading man was James Rennie. Her performance as Connie, the small town seamstress who waits patiently for her sailor over a period of two or three years, was poignant and very winning. There was something about her warm personality, and her forthright playing of the role, that was very engaging.

It was just a bit over twenty years before I saw her again. This time was on 1 February, 1943, at the National Theatre in Washington, D. C. The play was CLAUDIA, with Dorothy McGuire and Donald Cook as the stars. Here Miss Starr played the mother of the young bride, Claudia, who was a very naive girl at the time of her marriage. She learns that she is pregnant at the same time that she discovers that her mother is dying of cancer. The realization that she must learn to live without her mother manages to shock her into maturity. Miss Starr was again at her best in this role. The years had been kind and she still looked lovely. She played the role with great understanding and emotional appeal. She was very realistic and never seemed to be overly possessive. One final note is important here, too. On the cover of the program, where the stars' pictures usually appear, it was Frances Starr's picture that greeted the playgoer.

I wish that I might have seen her in many of her great roles, especially in THE EASIEST WAY, but I am happy that I saw her at least twice.

FRED STONE

This beloved American actor and musical comedy star has had a long and impressive career. Before my time, he had a twenty-two year partnership with David Montgomery. Together Montgomery and Stone toured the world, and they became international favorites until Mr. Montgomery's death in 1917. After a period in which Fred Stone mourned the loss of his great friend and co-star, he returned to the stage alone, and he became famous all over again.

I saw Fred Stone for the first time on 30 March, 1925, at the Illinois Theatre in Chicago. The play was STEPPING STONES, so titled because it was the first time that his talented older daughter, Dorothy Stone, was with him. Together they made history in a very amusing musical play. Most remembered were their scenes together, "Wonderful Dad", "Raggedy Ann", and "Stepping Stones", the latter a very amusing dance routine.

I saw him next on 1 December, 1930, at the Grand Opera House in Cincinnati. This time it was a musical based very lightly on "Rip Van Winkle"; it was called RIPPLES. Both Dorothy Stone, and his younger daughter, Paula Stone, were with him this time. The trio gave wonderful performances, and the show was amusing and tuneful. Fred Stone, was, of course cast as Rip. Best numbers were "I Take after Rip" with Dorothy Stone, and a very amusing "Cane Dance".

Two years later, I saw him again, on 22 February, 1932, again at the Grand Opera House in Cincinnati. This was called SMILING FACES, and only Paula Stone was with him this time. Dorothy Stone had gone on her own, and she was achieving quite a bit of fame and glory. In this show the numbers that I recall are: "Do Something Different", another "Cane Dance", and "Boot Black Blues" which was done with Paula Stone.

It was eleven years before I saw him again, and this was, unfortunately, the last time. This was on 6 July, 1943, at the National Theatre in Washington, D. C. Now he had decided to do a straight play. It was in a revival of one of our funniest comedies of the last few years, YOU CAN'T TAKE IT WITH YOU. As Martin Vanderhoff he gave a nostalgic bit of acting of the old school, but he was more Fred Stone than he was the character he was playing. After all, he was never considered to be a great actor; and there were moments in which he had great humility, especially in his final speech to the mad family and to the young couple who hoped to get married. He still had the Fred Stone charm. Bobbe Arnst was also in the cast.

His death a few years ago closed a very remarkable career in our theatre.

MARGARET SULLAVAN

In the short period of years in which Margaret Sullavan appeared on our stage, she has left us with a very clear memory of her ability.

Again my old friend, Ray Walsh, comes into these essays. It was he who told me the following story. He knew her when she was working in a Boston book store, and hers was a long and hard road. There were long periods in which she was unable to get a job in the theatre. There was summer stock, and her unfortunate marriage to Henry Fonda, then many tries in short-lived plays in New York. By the time that she had a good role in Kaufman and Ferber's STAGE DOOR, she had finally arrived.

All of these trials and troubles were behind her when I saw her first. By now she was an established star. This occurred on 2 January, 1944, at the Morosco Theatre in New York. The play was THE VOICE OF THE TURTLE. This was a very delightful comedy of the overtones of the war years. It had great appeal for a wide public, and it had a long run in New York. It was a three character play, and Elliott Nugent and Audrey Christie gave her excellent support. While it was not a great play it did have all of the elements of success. Miss Sullavan gave a winning and very appealing performance. Her low and well-modulated voice was one of her greatest assets.

Nearly ten years went by before I saw her again, and, unhappily it was for the last time. During these years she had gone through many personal problems, and she had been raising a family in her lovely home in Connecticut. This final time came on 20 April, 1953, at the Cox Theatre in Cincinnati. Incidentally, this was her first as well as her only appearance in our town. The play was THE DEEP BLUE SEA by Terrence

Rattigan. Here she was cast as a confused and insecure woman married to a fine but somewhat dull man. She had fallen deeply and hopelessly in love with a young aviator who was charming, but just as insecure as she. The tragedy of the play lies in her not knowing where to turn in her mixed-up life--thus the title of the play "between the devil and the deep blue sea". Suicide seemed to be the only answer, and how this was finally resolved was the theme of the play. Margaret Sullavan's performance had warmth and great pathos, and one left the theatre knowing that he had seen a very fine actress.

A few years later, when she was rehearsing for a new play, she discovered that her hearing had become impaired to the extent that she was unable to hear others on the stage, and therefore she missed many cues. Her tragic death, from accidentally taking an overdose of sleeping pills, was a great loss to our theatre. She had so much to give. We still miss her.

LAURETTE TAYLOR

It is hard to write about one of the truly great actresses of our time, when I must admit that I only saw her twice. However, I was fortunate to see her at a time when she was at her very best. In her early years, Laurette Taylor's career was spent in roles that she rarely ever appeared in out of New York. She became one of our finest actresses in roles that fitted her special talents, such as her long association through several revivals of PEG O' MY HEART and others. Then there came a dark period in her life in which, after the death of her husband, Hartly Manners, she went into retirement and into a period of decline. Through these years I always hoped that, somehow, she would return, and be able to relive again, for a new and anxious public, the very great ability that she had to give. Fortunately for me, and I am sure for many others, this did come true.

I saw her, for the first time, on 26 June, 1939, at the Playhouse Theatre in New York. The play was a revival of OUTWARD BOUND. In this production Bramwell Fletcher played Mr. Prior. Miss Taylor's entrance as Mrs. Midget will long remain in my memory. Here was a great actress appearing once more in a really fine role. She gave the part warmth, understanding, love, and humility. It was a beautiful performance. She brought tears to my eyes in the scene with her son, to whom she did not want to reveal her real identity.

Six years later I saw her again, for the last time. This was on 5 March, 1945, at the Civic Theatre in Chicago. This was in the pre-Broadway tryouts of Tennessee Williams' THE GLASS MENAGERIE. Her performance as Amanda Wingfield has now become a legend in our theatre. There were moments in which she gave to the role a quality of "lostness", a feeling of vagueness, memories of a southern belle of an older generation, that will always remain unforgettable. Two moments stand out in my memory: the pathetic telephone conversation when she is trying to sell subscriptions to a magazine to her friends; and the moment when she is out on the fire escape and looks at the moon through the tenement buildings that surround her. Eddie Dowling and Julie Hayden gave her fine support, but it was her evening in every way.

Her death on 7 December, 1946, closed the life of one of our greatest actresses. Fortunately, her daughter's book, LAURETTE, serves a much needed understanding of Miss Taylor's long career; and it allows us to see the real woman, with all of the many problems that she mastered with such great fortitude.

MARIE TEMPEST

There is quite a story about Marie Tempest. All of my theatre-going career was seemingly unfinished because I had never seen this great favorite. Her few American appearances had been many years ago, most of them before my time. However, I had followed her appearances in London, and I had read the wonderful biography that Hector Bolitho had written about her (published in 1937); and I had seen the one film in which she had appeared, THE MOONLIGHT SONATA.

To say that I went all the way to London to see her in her last play would not be quite true. However, let us say that I planned a trip to England at the time that she was playing in London. I suppose that it really adds up to the same thing.

Anyway, I saw Marie Tempest, finally, in July of 1939, at the Queen's Theatre in London. The play was DEAR OCTOPUS, a play which Dodie Smith had written especially for her. It was a delightful play about a couple on their fiftieth wedding anniversary having their children and grandchildren home to help celebrate the event. Somehow the family ties are strong enough to bring them home, even though all has not gone too well in the intervening years. The cast was as nearly perfect as one could wish. It included Leon Quatermaine as the husband, Charles, Hugh Williams as the favorite son, Angela Baddeley as the wayward daughter. But Miss Tempest, as Dora Randolph, was the star of the evening! It was hard to imagine, as I sat in a front stall, that this gracious and lovely woman was seventy-five years old. Even though she was wisely playing a woman of her own age, there was never a moment that her great talent for comedy and for humility did not shine through. Her curtain call, as I remember, was as gracious as a bubble and no one could even think of her age. This performance has always remained a treasured memory in all of my many years of theatre-going.

She didn't survive the Second World War years and this was, perhaps, just as well. She died quietly at her lovely home outside London on 15 October, 1942.

SYBIL THORNDYKE

This great British actress, whom I have always considered to be a "British Mrs. Fiske" has had a career spanning fifty or sixty years. She is a very great actress in serious drama or in comedy. There is something about her clipped speech, always clear and able to be heard in the farthest galleries, that has caused me to compare her with our great American actress, Mrs. Fiske, of another era in our theatre. She is small of stature, but wise and disciplined in her trade. She commands attention in every line that she speaks.

I saw her only once. The date was in July, 1939 at the Duchess Theatre in London. The play was THE CORN IS GREEN. Along with Emlyn Williams she made this a great achievement. Her Miss Moffat was a complete joy to watch and to hear. She had humility and warmth.

Miss Thorndyke has appeared many times in the United States, but it has never been my good fortune to see her. Surely it is my loss.

SOPHIA TUCKER

The death of Sophie Tucker yesterday (10 February, 1966), at seventy-eight, brings back many memories of this great entertainer. My memories cover a period of over forty years.

No dates are available, but for a period of the late 'teens through the early twenties, I saw her each year as a member of the vaudeville "bill" at the old Orpheum Theatre in Peoria. She always had top billing and the best "spot" on the program. Her songs sung in her brassy, throaty voice became a legend in her own time. She was loud and often vulgar in some of her songs, but somehow no one seemed to care as long as she was singing them. She was always resplendent in modish clothes of the period with many expensive jewels displayed to advantage.

The only time that I ever saw her in the "legit" was in a revue called "LES MAIRES AFFAIRES" at the Woods Theatre in Chicago. This was during the season of 1923-1924. It was a rather mediocre revue which had a short life. When she forgot that she was in a show, and became herself and sang her songs, the revue had excitement; in fact, she was the entire show. This didn't save the show, but it did give us Miss Tucker. Bobbe Arnst was also in the show, and she gave evidence of promise, but somehow she had a very short career in the theatre. I do not know why.

Many years passed before I saw Miss Tucker again. This time it was at the Beverley Hills Country Club, outside of Cincinnati, in the 1940's. In a regular night club act, she was again in her element. When she came on stage, ablaze in jewels and radiance of personality, singing "Some Of These Days", there was no stopping the applause and the cheers of the audience.

Her talent was unique in our entertainment world. "The Last of the Red Hot Mamas" was her beloved title, and she never let an audience down. With her passing, an entire era of American entertainment has gone. We shall miss her--she was an institution.

LENORE ULRIC

Lenore Ulric was a famous Belasco star. She had a trained sense of the dramatic. She was of dark complexion, and very sultry and seductive in her movements. But she did have glamour and a certain amount of talent. I mention all of these points because she was, in her day, a very prominent star. In all of her famous roles she was very vocal and theatrical. In no way was she ever a great actress; she was an interesting one, and I found myself drawn to the theatre to see her whenever she appeared.

I saw her first on Christmas Eve, 1923, at the Powers Theatre in Chicago. The play was KIKI, one of her greatest successes. As the French girl of the streets, she was in her element. Sam Hardy and Thomas Mitchell gave her excellent support.

I saw her next, during the season of 1927, at the Illinois Theatre in Chicago. The play was LULU BELLE, perhaps her greatest success. As the negro strumpet, she was again having a field day. It was staged with true Belasco realism, and, as a stage piece, it was interesting. It was pure melodrama, and in any other hands it would have had a very short career. With Lenore Ulric, and Belasco, it was a great commercial hit. Chester Morris was her luckless paramour.

I didn't see her again for eight years, during which time her career was on the wane, and none of her shows were the successes they used to be. This was on 21 January, 1935, at the Shubert Theatre in Cincinnati. The play was PAGAN LADY, which turned out to be a rather weak rehash of all of the other roles she had played through the years. It was a rather sad occasion.

Many years went by and I had lost all track of Miss Ulric, when, lo and behold, she turned up in the cast of Katharine Cornell's ANTHONY AND CLEOPATRA playing the role of Charmain. I saw it first at the Emery Auditorium in Cincinnati on 27 October, 1947, and again at Fords' Theatre in Baltimore. Gone were most of the histrionics and the posing of old, and, in their place, she had gained wisdom and depth. Her performance was disciplined, and in good taste. In the final scene she was very moving.

Miss Ulric died in 1970.

JUNE WALKER

The death, a year ago in February, 1966 of June Walker reminded me of the many times I had seen this very capable and charming actress. My memories of Miss Walker go back forty years when she was a delightful ingenue and was just coming into the stardom which she gained after long, hard work in the theatre.

I first saw June Walker on 6 June, 1926, at the Selwyn Theatre in Chicago. The play was GENTLEMEN PREFER BLONDES which was made from Anita Loos' delightful book, a best seller in those far-away days. Since Miss Walker was not a blonde, she seemed a strange choice for Loreli. However, any of us oldsters who saw that performance realized that no one else could have played the role. She was so absolutely right for the part and the fact that she wore a blonde wig was utterly unimportant. She made this most implausible but highly amusing character her very own. She was in the show for a long, long time. Edna Hibbard and Frank Morgan were in her cast.

By the time that I saw her next, on 25 February, 1929, at the Grand Theatre in Cincinnati, she had come a long way, and she was now in a Belasco production. If she was not actually being made into a Belasco star, at least she was in one of his best and most amusing productions. The play was THE BACHELOR FATHER. As Tony Flagg, one of the several illegitimate children of a certain Sir Basil Winterton of Rooksfold house, an estate in England, she was giving one of her most charming performances. It was a very well-written comedy, and it was played with good taste as well as good humor. I remember it with much amusement. C. Aubrey Smith was wonderful as Sir Basil and Geoffrey Kerr was the young man who admired and finally won Tony.

When I saw her next it was on 17 October, 1932, at the Shubert Theatre in Cincinnati. The play was THE PURE IN HEART. This was one of those plays with a message, and with overtones of a socialized society. Neither the message nor the social uplift seemed to come across the footlights with much strength of purpose, and certainly with very little drama. It was a pre-Broadway performance. Osgood Perkins and Paul Kelly were both in the cast, and they, along with Miss Walker, had all left the cast before the play opened in New York.

It was almost ten years before I saw June Walker again. This time it was April, 1941, at the Taft Theatre in Cincinnati. This was her only try at Shakespeare, to the best of my knowledge. She played the Maria in the Helen Hayes--Maurice Evans production of TWELFTH NIGHT. Her characterization was in the best Shakespearean tradition, and she gave to the role all the ribald humor that the part demands. She was coy, vivacious, and a complete delight. The scenes in which she was plotting all of the masterful tricks on the luckless Malvolio were cleverly played, and with great wit. She was also a perfect bar maid in the Tavern scene.

The last time that I saw June Walker was in the National Company with Thomas Mitchell in Arthur Miller's DEATH OF A SALESMAN. This I saw at the Erlanger Theatre in Chicago on 28 December, 1949. As Lind Loman, the wife of Willy Loman, she had dignity and humility. She was more "womanly" than Mildred Dunock, whom I had seen in New York with Lee Cobb. While I still feel that Miss Dunock was the better actress in this particular role, Miss Walker gave a very moving performance.

Yes, I have many happy memories of June Walker.

Miss Walker died in 1969.

DAVID WARFIELD

For the first twenty-five years of the twentieth century, one of the most beloved actors, as well as one of the most popular, was David Warfield. The historians and the critics who write about this period in the American theatre tell us that he came out of San Francisco as a nobody, and in a few short years with David Belasco he became one of our most famous stars.

I saw him for the first time at the Majestic Theatre in Peoria, during the season of 1919, when he was on tour with THE AUCTIONEER. This was one of his most famous roles, and I recall how much I enjoyed its homely humor and pathos. My memories are dim, but I do recall the quiet dignity of his performance. (Marie Bates, who was with him, had been in his company for many years.)

I next saw Mr. Warfield on the night after Christmas, 26 December, 1921, at the Powers Theatre in Chicago. It was the opening night of his revival of THE RETURN OF PETER GRIMM. I can still hear the great ovation that he received from the packed audience when he first appeared. This was a dream play with a great deal of understanding of love and humility. In his usual manner, at the final curtain he seemed to bring everything back to happiness for all. It was a memorable performance.

After many years in the theatre, as his career was coming to a close, Mr. Warfield had a chance to do the one Shakespearean role which he had always wanted to do, the one for which he was most obviously fitted. This was, of course, Shylock, in THE MERCHANT OF VENICE. I saw it on 14 December, 1923, at the Illinois Theatre in Chicago. Perhaps his characterization of this famous role was a bit too humane, and perhaps he played the role more for sympathy than the hatred that one finds in the

GENEVIEVE TOBIN

Genevieve Tobin is an actress who, some years ago, was in most popular favor. She has charm, wit, and a good sense of comedy. She retired from the stage over thirty years ago, and today she is one of the managers of a large Theatre Party Booking Management in New York.

I saw her for the first time on 1 January, 1921, at the Cohans' Grand Opera House in Chicago. The play was LITTLE OLD NEW YORK. It was a play set in a period of days gone by, around the turn of the century, and it was played with a great deal of nostalgia. Miss Tobin had great appeal, and it was an amusing play, as I recall. Ernest Glendenning was her leading man. He was a very popular actor in those days, and, as far as I know, this was the only time that I ever saw him.

I next saw Genevieve Tobin on 20 August, 1923, at the Little Theatre in New York. The play was POLLY PREFERRED. This was a play about women in the business world, and how one, in this case Miss Tobin, became the head of a large investment business. Again she was a delight. William Harrigan was her leading man.

The last time that I saw her was on 28 August, 1926, at the Harris Theatre in Chicago. She was trying out a play called TREAT 'EM ROUGH. This was a mistake, as it was a play of little consequence, and it had a very short life. The cast included Walter Connelly and George Gaul.

way some of the greater Shakespearean actors have played this role; he did, however, give it a great dignity. It was a heartening performance. Mary Servoss was Portia.

David Warfield lived many years in retirement, and was one of the wealthiest of our actors when he died on 27 June, 1951. In his own way, he represented a period in the American theatre which has long since evaporated from our view. I am happy that I saw him when he was at his best.

ETHEL WATERS

This very great woman has had many ups and downs in our theatre. She has reached the top on the musical as well as the legitimate stage. She has been acclaimed as one of our greatest actresses; she has torn at our heart strings when she has sung some of her torch songs; and yet, she has always been unstable. Fame has somehow been too much for her, and just as soon as she reaches the top, where she has been on several occasions, she slips back into oblivion. This has been one of the greatest tragedies in our modern theatre. Today, in the 1960's, she is again at her lowest ebb. My memories of Ethel Waters span thirty-four years, which is a long while in the theatre.

I saw Ethel Waters for the first time on 13 March, 1932, at the Shubert Theatre in Cincinnati. The musical was RHAPSODY IN BLACK. This was a very memorable musical. The cast also included The Berry Brothers who were excellent. One won't easily forget "What's Keeping my Prince Charming" nor "You Can't Stop Me From Loving You". Both were sung in her best style, and were show stoppers.

The next time that I saw Ethel Waters was on 31 March, 1934, at the Music Box Theatre in New York. The musical was AS THOUSANDS CHEER, in which she was in the good company of Marilyn Miller and Clifton Webb. This was a great revue, and her outstanding songs were "Supper Time" and "I've Got Rhythm On My Mind".

A little over a year later I saw her again, during Christmas week of 1935, at the Winter Garden Theatre in New York. The musical was AT HOME ABROAD, and this time she was in the good company of Beatrice Lillie and Eleanor Powell. Her most memorable numbers were "Hotentot Potentate",

"The Steamboat Whistle", and "Got A Bran' New Suit" which she sang to perfection while Eleanor Powell danced. It was a show stopping number, and they were both at their best.

She now longed for the legitimate theatre, and the dramatic roles which she knew that she could do, if she had the opportunity. Her first chance came within the next six years, and I saw her on 12 November, 1940, at the Taft Theatre in Cincinnati. The play was MAMBA'S DAUGHTERS. In this play she was the ultimate of tragedy, and her pathos and understanding of the role were outstanding. She had arrived as a great dramatic actress; she had reached one of the goals that she had set for herself. It was a great achievement.

However, she returned to the musical stage when she found just the right part. This chance came quite soon. In it she reached her highest peak in the musical world. The show was, of course, CABIN IN THE SKY. I saw it on 23 June, 1941, at the Curran Theatre in San Francisco. She had a wonderful supporting cast which included Todd Duncan, Rex Ingram, and Katherine Dunham. It was a very high point in musical theatre. I was in San Francisco on a vacation, and I felt that I must see this show, but all of the seats were sold out. However, the management decided to put in a row of chairs, and I was fortunate to get one of them. Therefore, from a chair placed about tenth row center, I was able to cheer Miss Waters on. Will anyone ever forget "Taking a Chance On Love" (which, by actual count, she had to repeat six times the night I was there)? It still rings in my memory as one of the great moments to remember in musical theatre, ranking along with "Old Man River" and "Bill" from SHOW BOAT. There were many other highlights in the show, especially Miss Dunham's dance numbers.

Twelve years went by before I saw her again. This time she was back in a dramatic role. She was winning the plaudits of the critics and public alike. This was her tremendous performance in THE MEMBER OF THE WEDDING. I saw it on 19 March, 1952, at the Cox Theatre in Cincinnati. I suppose of all of the achievements she has acquired in the American theatre, this was her greatest. It is a beautiful play and she gave to the role of Bernice all of the pent-up talent she had been saving all of these years. She gave to this very wonderful character fidelity and love. It was a fitting climax to a great career.

She has made some night club appearances since then, and I was fortunate to see her once more at the Beverly Hills Country Club outside Cincinnati during the season 1957-58. She was in fine form and she sang many of the old favorites. However, she soon disappeared into oblivion again, and during the past ten years or so she has done very little. From my own personal point of view, I think that this is a great waste. With her great talent she had everything to offer, and many of us would be happy to welcome her back, and would give her our love and admiration.

DAME MAY WHITTY

This character actress was much loved by a wide public, both on the stage and in a series of well-remembered films. She had great wit, and she was a fine comedienne.

I saw her first on 29 April, 1932, at Henry Miller's Theatre in New York. The play was THERE'S ALWAYS JULIET, starring Edna Best and Herbert Marshall. Here she was the kindly housekeeper who aided and helped along the sudden romance. She had a quick use of gestures, and a very quiet way of underplaying a line.

I saw her next in London, at the Duchess Theatre, during the summer of 1936. The play was NIGHT MUST FALL, a play by Emlyn Williams in which he also appeared. She was the older woman who was confined to a wheel chair, and she was the focal point of the play. Her sudden fright at outsiders, and the way in which she accepted the false attentions of the "bell hop", gave her a field day in acting. She had a certain dignity in everything that she played.

She soon journeyed over to the United States again, and I saw her for the last time on 29 November, 1937, at the Cox Theatre in Cincinnati. Here she was in a play called YOU'RE OBEDIENT HUSBAND. It was a play that had little substance, and this was a pre-Broadway tour. It starred Frederic March and Florence Eldridge. It had an idea, but it was poorly written. Dame May gave it her best, but none of the cast had very much to do, and its run in New York was very brief.

Her daughter, Margaret Webster, has become one of our finest directors, and she has also appeared infrequently on our stage. Dame May Whitty died quietly on 29 May, 1948. She will be remembered by a large and faithful following.

MRS. THOMAS WHIFFEN

Mrs. Thomas Whiffen was one of the most lovable of old ladies. She, of course, belonged to the old school of actresses who used their married names in the theatre. She never achieved fame as a star, but she was always the most important member of the supporting cast. Frequently her name was on the program along with whoever was the star of that particular play. She usually played grandmothers, with a winning and winsome manner.

I saw her first at the Majestic Theatre in Peoria, on 16 February, 1920. The play was STEVE. It starred Eugene O'Brien who had been, and still was at that time, a very popular leading man in the films. It was his only major appearance on the legitimate stage. He had personality and charm, but he was never much of an actor. Mrs. Whiffen was "Granny", and I recall that their scenes together were played with fun and understanding, and that she was the more seasoned actress.

The next time that I saw Mrs. Whiffen was at the Blackstone Theatre in Chicago. This was during the season of 1923. The play was JUST SUPPOSE, which starred Patricia Collinge and Leslie Howard. Here, she was Mrs. Carter Stafford, the mother. Born and bred in true southern tradition, she gave the role a certain quality which made it stand out even with the major stars having the leading roles.

The last time that I saw Mrs. Whiffen was on 20 June, 1924, at the Bijou Theatre in New York. I had just graduated from high school, and was on a graduation trip with my cousins. This night had a very amusing memory also. I had been taking a walk around Times Square, and I was passing the theatre just as the first intermission was letting out. It was a warm night, before air conditioning so that the sidewalk was crowded. As a lark, I went into the theatre with the crowd--and no one bothered me as to a ticket stub--so, I sat in a rear seat in the orchestra and saw the rest of the play. It was THE GOOSE HANGS HIGH, a very clever comedy of American life with the grandchildren causing no end of problems. The stars were Norman Trevor and Katherine Grey as the distraught parents. Mrs. Whiffen was again the grandmother who had more sympathy and understanding of the teen age problem than did the parents. It has long been a very popular play for all age groups in the amateur field.

Shortly after this performance Mrs. Whiffen retired from the stage. She died quietly on 25 November, 1936.

ESTELLE WINWOOD

Estelle Winwood is now, at this writing, eighty-four years old. During the past year, or so, she was a guest star with the Cleveland Playhouse, and was in a short-lived play in New York. What a woman! What a wonderful life! She has been entertaining countless thousands throughout a long and varied career. Her overflowing sense of humor, her perfect timing, and her big, wide eyes have been the things that we all remember.

I saw Miss Winwood for the first time on 20 October, 1930, at the Shubert Theatre in Cincinnati. The play was SCARLET SISTER MARY which starred Ethel Barrymore. She played the role of Cindy, and even her good humor could not save this poorly-constructed play. I was at once impressed, however, as I had heard of her for many years.

The next time I saw her was in Chicago, at the Harris Theatre, in February, 1938. Here I was able to see her in three different roles, on Friday night, Saturday matinee, and Saturday evening, in the entire series of Noel Coward's TONIGHT AT EIGHT-THIRTY. Her variety was amazing. I especially recall Lavinia Featherways in FAMILY ALBUM, Doris Gow in FUMED OAK (outstanding), and her peculiar humor was at its best as Lady Maureen Gilpin in HANDS ACROSS THE SEA. Bramwell Fletcher and the lovely Helen Chandler were also in this cast.

In June of 1940, I saw her next at the Henry Miller Theatre in New York. This was in LADIES IN RETIREMENT starring Flora Robson. As one of the mad sisters who was always "tidying up the beach", she gave one of the funniest performances I have ever seen.

The next time that I saw Estelle Winwood was on 1 October, 1942, at the Taft Theatre in Cincinnati. I was on leave from the U. S. Navy, and I had come home for a few days. The play was THE PIRATE which starred the Lunts. She had little to do, but she was fun to watch anyway. As always, she made you well aware that she was on the stage, even in a show that was written for this famous couple.

I saw her next at the Cort Theatre in New York, on 3 April, 1947. This was in the all-star revival of LADY WINDEMERE'S FAN. As the Duchess of Berwick, in this old museum piece, she was having a field day, and she was at her superlative best. It remains very vivid in my memory. The cast included Cornelia Otis Skinner, Penelope Dudley Ward, John Buckmaster, and David Manners. It was a rare theatrical treat, as this old play seemed as new as if it had just been written.

Two years later, on 4 March, 1949, I saw her again, at the Belasco Theatre in New York. This was in THE MAD WOMAN OF CHAILLOT starring Martita Hunt. As Mme. Constance she was as "fey" as ever, and she made the role stand out. John Carridine and Leora Dana were also in this cast. A year later, on 8 May, 1950, I saw this play again, at the Cox Theatre in Cincinnati. She was still in the cast, and as mad as ever. It was at this time that I saw her "off stage". I happened to drop in late one evening at one of the more popular bars around town, and there she was, perched on a bar stool, in her big picture hat not quite covering those wide eyes, and, as always, surrounded by a bevy of young men. She was just as theatrical off stage as she ever was on stage.

Ten years went by before I saw her again. This was in April, 1959 at the Shubert Theatre in Cincinnati. This was the last time that I saw her. The play was HERE TODAY, starring Tallulah Bankhead. This was a weak play which I had seen twenty-five or more years ago in Chicago with Ruth Gordon as the star. In this earlier production Miss Winwood's role was played by Charlotte Granville, another old-timer in the theatre. The years had not improved the play, and I was at a loss to understand why it had been revived at all. However, Miss Bankhead really bent over backward to give the entire show to Miss Winwood. She was wonderful, as she always was, and it was a joy to see her again.

Although she is now in partial retirement, one hopes that we may be able to see her one more time.

PEGGY WOOD

Peggy Wood has had a long and most varied career in our theatre. She is able to play almost anything. In her youth she was a musical comedy star, and this continued for many years. Then she turned to straight drama, and in both mediums she has been successful. My memories of Peggy Wood cover a period of forty-five years. I have been fortunate, too, because I have seen her in both facets of her career, and I have enjoyed her performances very much.

My programs tell me that I saw Miss Wood for the first time during the season of 1920 at the Woods Theatre in Chicago. This musical was BUDDIES, a most entertaining show with overtones of the First World War. She was supported by Donald Brian and Ralph Morgan. She was singing beautifully.

I saw her next on 6 September, 1925, at the Princess Theatre, again in Chicago. Here she was playing in Bernard Shaw's CANDIDA. Her Candida was filled with great humility, and with a marvelous sense of humor. She gave to the role all of the womanly qualities that made it most believeable. Morgan Farley was the Marchbanks, and this was the finest performance I ever saw him give.

Nineteen years went by before I saw Peggy Wood again. This was on 20 January, 1944, at Fords' Theatre in Baltimore. The play was Noel Coward's wonderful farce, BLITHE SPIRIT. Along with Haila Stoddard, Clifton Webb, and Mildred Natwick, Miss Wood was having a marvelous time. This quartette gave to Mr. Coward's best play all of the humor and nonsense that it needed. It was an evening full of fun.

Another fifteen years went by before I saw Peggy Wood for the last time. This was on 1 April, 1959, at the Civic Theatre in Chicago. The play was THE GIRLS IN 509. This proved to be one of the funniest comedies I had seen in a long while. Miss Wood, along with Imogene Coca, gave the show a tremendous satirical performance. The plot, such as it was, about two women who had remained in their hotel suite ever since FDR had been elected, was a masterful job of spoofing.

It was so good to see her as the Mother Superior in the film version of THE SOUND OF MUSIC. She had great dignity, as well as her wonderful sense of humor.

HAIDEE WRIGHT

Although I saw Haidee Wright only twice, and both times late in her career, I was fascinated by her. She had a peculiar way of making any role that she was playing especially her own. Both times she was entirely different; there was never a "sameness" about her.

I saw her for the first time on 22 April, 1929, at the Shubert Theatre in Cincinnati. The play was THE ROYAL FAMILY. This play which was so cleverly written by George Kaufman and Edna Ferber about the Barrymore family, was a delight. With its three generations of one family who had been on the stage, it gave a very fine picture of theatre. Haidee Wright's performance as Fanny was outstanding, and one that I shall long remember. She was so right for the part, and her sure theatrical sense made her even more effective. She was supported by most of the original cast, including Otto Kruger, Ann Andrews, and Ferdinand Gottchalk.

Just a little over a year later, I saw her on 22 December, 1930, at the Charles Hopkins Theatre in New York. The play was MRS. MOONLIGHT starring Edith Barret, Sir Guy Standing, and Leo G. Carroll. She had a relatively minor role of the faithful servant. She rarely left her perch on a high stool, but she commanded every scene that she was in. It was a quaint play, full of mystery and charm.

I heard very little of her after this performance and, unfortunately, I never saw her again. In 1942 I read of her death on 29 January of that year. Her's was a unique place in our theatre.

ED WYNN

Ed Wynn has been a national institution in the American theatre for over fifty years. The infectious laugh, the simple, almost child-like little voice, the marvelous buffoonery have long been landmarks in our musical theatre lore. One can hardly ever remember any of his productions being pure musical comedy as there was very little plot--just Mr. Wynn having a wonderful time entertaining his thousands of admirers.

My own memories of Ed Wynn cover a period of forty-five years. I was first enchanted by his complete abandon on 21 April, 1922, at the Majestic Theatre in Peoria. This was called ED WYNN CARNIVAL, and it was well named. It was just that. In most of the numbers, as I recall from the program, he was listed as "By Himself", and he gave much amusement with his fooling.

I saw him next, six years later, on 9 December, 1928, at the Shubert Theatre in Cincinnati. The play was MANHATTAN MARY. This one did have some semblance of plot as he was cast as Crickets. The most remembered scenes are: "Ma Brennan's Lunch Room", in which he was very funny; "A Secluded Spot", in which he brought out many of his wonderful gadgets and inventions; and a very funny dance routine number, in which he danced with Nick Long, Jr.

I saw him next on 20 November, 1932, again at the Shubert Theatre in Cincinnati. The play was THE LAUGH PARADE. Here the style was the same as always, and he went on from place to place. These places are amusingly listed in my program in the following manner: "As an Acrobat in a Familiar Place", "As a Bench Sitter in a Nice Place", and "As a Fireman in a Foolish Place". They were all hilarious.

I saw Ed Wynn for the last time on 23 October, 1941, at the Taft Theatre in Cincinnati. This was called BOYS AND GIRLS TOGETHER. Throughout he was "Boy" in a variety of amusing scenes, always surrounded by a bevy of beautiful girls. His clowning was superb. As one of our great American comedians, he stands alone. He never had the subtlety of W. C. Fields, nor the drollery of Charles Butterworth, but he has always succeeded in what he set out to do--to make his audiences laugh. He could never sing like Al Jolson, nor like Eddie Cantor, but somehow that never seemed to matter.

I have seen him many times since then on T. V., and have heard him through the years on radio. Just past seventy he began a completely new role for himself in the films. He turns up from time to time, and in even a small scene in which he appears, he always steals the show.

Mr. Wynn died, in the summer of 1966, in Hollywood.

DIANA WYNWARD

When, during the season of 1964-1965, I read of the sudden and untimely death of Diana Wynward, I felt a great loss to our theatre. Miss Wynward possessed a certain quality that was especially her own. She had haunting beauty, quiet charm, and a special grace. I was most fortunate to see her as many times as I did, and for that I am very grateful. It all began when she was a very young actress at the time she was first appearing in the United States. This was at the Selwyn Theatre in Chicago. The date was 9 May, 1932. The play was THE DEVIL PASSES. It was a somewhat strange play with overtones of mysticism that confused many in the audience. However, it told a quite simple story of The Prince of Darkness, a young curate passing through an English parish, who paused long enough to expose the virtues of the muddled souls he found there rather than to expose their sins. It was heart-warming in every sense. The American managers had surrounded Miss Wynward with a top flight cast which included Arthur Byron, Mary Nash, Robert Lorraine, with Basil Rathbone as the curate. It is interesting, too, that never again did I see Diana Wynward in the United States.

I saw her next on 27 July, 1936, four years later, at the Kings' Theatre in Edinburgh, Scotland. The play was THE ANTE-ROOM. This was a play of family differences and feuds which was perfectly staged, and had moments of great beauty; but it never really caught on, and its run in London a few weeks later was brief. Miss Wynward had grown tremendously in her ability to create a character, and she did all that she could in a rather dull play. This time, also, she had a very outstanding cast, including Jessica Tandy, Morland Graham, and Marius Goring. It was produced and directed by Guthrie McClintic as a possible choice for Katharine Cornell in the United States, but it was never produced over here.

I saw her again the following summer, this time at the Theatre Des Champs Elysees in Paris. The date was 12 July, 1937. She had come over from London during the World's Fair for a brief appearance to represent the British Theatre. The play was George Bernard Shaw's CANDIDA. I have seen many actresses play Candida, over a period of years, and I was much touched and excited over her performance. She gave it a warmth and humility and a wise understanding that the role must have. It was a glorious performance. She was most ably supported by Nicholas Hannen and Stephen Haggard, as Morell and Marchbanks respectively.

I saw her next in London at the Queen's Theatre in July of 1938. This was in one of her most famous roles, in SWEET AHOLES. It was a pure sentimental drama of the old school, but she made it far more than that. Again she had a certain warmth and dignity that the role needed. It was a heart-warming performance.

I last saw Miss Wynward in July, 1939, in London at the Savoy Theatre. She was having a romp in Noel Coward's DESIGN FOR LIVING. She played the role of Gilda quite differently from the way it had been played in the United States by Lynn Fontanne, but she made it her own, and it was filled with humor and understanding. She was supported by Rex Harrison and Anton Walbrook, both of whom were most competent actors. It still had the completely inane quality of the original, and it was good fun.

Of her many appearances in the films, I don't suppose that I shall ever forget her in CALVACADE. Here she demonstrated all of her great gifts as an actress.

I am sorry that I did not see her last American appearance in Shaw's HEARTBREAK HOUSE (which happens to be one of my favorite plays) but I understand from friends who did see it that she was as lovely as ever. Yes, we shall miss Diana Wynward. Her career was all too brief.

ROLAND YOUNG

Roland Young was another of our major actors who died much too soon. I was shocked to read of his death a few years ago. He seemed to be always the same, and his personality was overflowing with good humor. He was a man who was a great comedian, and one who seemed to give his best to every role that he played.

I saw Roland Young first on 23 August, 1923, at the Garrick Theatre in New York. The play was George Bernard Shaw's THE DEVIL'S DISCIPLE. He played General Burgoyne, and, while it was not the lead role, it was a very funny characterization. I thought then that here was a man that I should hope to see again. The play was well cast with the following: Basil Sydney as Richard Dudgeon, and Caroll McComas as Judith Anderson, the wife of the Reverend Anderson.

I saw him next, a little over a year later, on 8 September, 1924, at the Adelphi Theatre in Chicago. Now he was playing Neil McCrae, the leading role in BEGGAR ON HORSEBACK. This was a charming play of man against his dream world. It was a great deal of fun to watch. Here he was at his best. He was supported by Spring Byington and Osgood Perkins, who are already mentioned elsewhere in these memoirs.

Three years went by before I saw him again. This time was also in Chicago, at the Blackstone Theatre, during the season of 1927. The play was THE LAST OF MRS. CHEYNEY, in which he played Lord Arthur Dilling opposite Ina Claire. His droll humor was never more evident than it was in this delightful comedy. It was a highlight in his long career.

I next saw Roland Young on 12 November, 1928, at the Shubert Theatre in Cincinnati. The play was THE QUEEN'S HUSBAND. This was an amusing bit of intrigue within a mythical Royal Family in an unknown country. It was hugely entertaining. Marie Adels was with him.

It was twenty-five years before I saw him again, and, unfortunately, it was for the last time. The date was 27 September, 1943, at the National Theatre in Washington, D. C. The play was ANOTHER LOVE STORY. Although it was written by Frederick Lonsdale, it did not have the flair that he had given us in his earlier comedies. However, it was fun, and Mr. Young was, again, at his urbane best. He was supported by Margaret Lindsay who had been well-known in the films.

Naturally I had seen him many times in the films that he had made over the years. Who can forget his Uriah Heep in the film of DAVID COPPERFIELD, or his many zany films with Billie Burke? Roland Young has not been replaced by any of our newer actors, and I doubt that he ever will be. His talent was unique, and it is doubtful that anyone can ever quite achieve his special qualities.

www.ingramcontent.com/pod-product-compliance
Lightning Source LLC
Chambersburg PA
CBHW080439170426
43195CB00017B/2828